MONEY MINDSET -AWAKENED-

The Key to Achieving Next-Level Wealth

Choyo Gomex

TABLE OF CONTENTS

PROLOGUE 3
INTRODUCTION 6
CHAPTER 1 12
The Awakening: Recognizing Money as Energy 12
CHAPTER 2 22
Mental Blocks Identifying and Overcoming Limiting Beliefs 22
CHAPTER 3 34
The Subconscious Blueprint Reprogramming for Wealth 34
CHAPTER 4 42
The Neuroscience of Wealth Training Your Brain for Prosperity 42
CHAPTER 5 54
The Power of Focus Directing Mental Energy Toward Wealth Creation 54
CHAPTER 6 66
Financial Visualization Manifesting Wealth Through Mental Imagery 66
CHAPTER 7 75
Cultivating Abundance Shifting from Scarcity to Limitless Thinking 75
CHAPTER 8 87
The Power of Tithing, Giving to Receive Abundance 87
CHAPTER 8 92
Emotional Mastery Aligning Feelings with Financial Goals 92
CHAPTER 9 104
Intuition and Money Tapping into Your Inner Wealth Guide 104
CHAPTER 10 113
The Awakened Mindset Living in Alignment with Abundance 113
BONUS CHAPTER 121
BITCOIN The Digital Revolution of Money and Wealth Creation 121
REFERENCES 138

PROLOGUE

Awakening to the Power of Your Money Mindset

Imagine for a moment that your mind is the foundation upon which all your financial success is built. Every decision, every action, and every opportunity that comes your way is influenced by your thoughts, beliefs, and emotions about money. Your mind, in essence, is the engine that drives your financial life, and how you think about money can either propel you forward or hold you back.

Many people navigate their financial journey without realizing their mindset's profound impact on their success. They may set goals, work hard, or even stumble upon moments of economic gain. However, their deep-seated beliefs about money—formed by experiences, societal conditioning, and subconscious programming—determine the ceiling of their financial potential.

The good news is that your financial reality doesn't have to be dictated by outdated beliefs, past failures, or inherited limitations. With the right mindset, you can unlock new levels of abundance and prosperity and awaken the immense power of your thoughts and emotions in shaping your financial destiny.

This book is your guide to transforming your money mindset and, in doing so, reprogramming your mind for financial success. Whether you're seeking to increase your wealth, break free from financial struggles, or develop a healthier relationship with money, the journey begins with recognizing the power of your mind.

The Role of Your Money Mindset

A money mindset isn't just about having positive thoughts or wishing for financial abundance. It's about consciously shaping your beliefs, attitudes, and emotional responses to money to align with your desired economic success. It's about understanding that money, at its core, is energy—a tool that flows into your life based on how you manage that energy mentally and emotionally.

For many, the first step toward financial empowerment is identifying the mental blocks and limiting beliefs that keep them from reaching their goals. These mental blocks often stem from past experiences, cultural conditioning, and subconscious programming. Perhaps you grew up hearing that "money is the root of all evil" or that "wealth is only for the lucky or the privileged." These beliefs can create invisible barriers, preventing you from fully stepping into your financial potential.

By reprogramming your subconscious mind and learning to master your thoughts and emotions, you can remove these barriers. You can cultivate a mindset that attracts wealth and allows you to manage and grow it sustainably. This transformation begins with the understanding that you can change how you think about money—and, by extension, your financial life.

Embracing the Journey of Financial Awakening

This book is not just about financial strategies or quick fixes. It's about awakening to the deeper truths about money, wealth, and abundance. You'll learn to recognize the unconscious patterns holding you back and replace them with empowering beliefs aligning with your financial goals.

From understanding the neuroscience of wealth to harnessing the power of visualization, from cultivating an abundance mindset to mastering your emotions—each chapter provides tools and insights to awaken your financial potential. As you move through the pages, you'll discover that economic success is not a distant dream but a reality you can create.

You'll also explore the importance of aligning your financial decisions with your core values, trusting your intuition, and developing a holistic approach to wealth-building. This journey is about more than just accumulating money; it's about achieving true financial freedom—the kind that allows you to live a life of purpose, joy, and abundance.

The Path Ahead

As you embark on this transformative journey, know that every step you take brings you closer to your financial goals. Whether you're looking to build wealth, achieve financial security, or break free from financial stress, the foundation of your success lies within your mind.

This book is your companion, offering practical guidance, powerful techniques, and inspirational insights to help you reprogram your mind for financial abundance. The lessons you'll learn here are timeless and applicable, whether you are just starting your financial journey or seeking to elevate your wealth to new heights.

Now is the time to awaken your money mindset, break free from limiting beliefs, and step into the financial life you've always dreamed of. Remember, the power to create wealth and abundance is already within you. It's time to unlock that power and live in alignment with the financial abundance that is your birthright.

INTRODUCTION

The Power of an Awakened Money Mindset

Welcome to the third book in this series, *Money Mindset Awakened: Your Guide to Achieve Next-Level Financial Freedom*. You've made it here, congratulations. You've already begun a profound journey toward financial mastery through practical steps and by shifting your mindset. Your proactive steps have set you on the path to financial freedom, and this book represents the next level of that transformation. Here, we'll dive deeper into the mental aspects of wealth, exploring the inner world that genuinely determines your financial reality. Your journey is hereby acknowledged and celebrated.

The first two books laid the foundation for understanding the power of mindset in wealth creation. *MONEY The Universal Language of Wealth* gave you insight into the essence of money, its origins, and how our perception of it influences our ability to accumulate it. We explored vital concepts such as the consciousness of money, the law of cause and effect, and how shifting your perspective can unlock new abundance levels. *The Money Blueprint* took you further by providing actionable strategies to activate your wealth mindset. We discussed the traits necessary for building wealth, the mechanics of cultivating a prosperous mindset, and techniques for rewiring your mind for financial success. Each chapter aims to help you take control of your financial future by reshaping your internal landscape.

But now, it's time to move beyond those foundational ideas. In *Money Mindset Awakened*, we will go even deeper into the mind's inner workings—uncovering how your thoughts, emotions, and beliefs shape your financial reality at every level. More importantly, we will awaken your latent potential to master money as a mental game.

Money is of the Mind, It's a Mental Game

You may have heard "money is a mental game," but what does that mean? For many, it sounds like a cliché, a catchphrase often thrown around without much substance. However, truly understanding the depth of this concept can revolutionize how you approach money forever.

At its core, the idea that money is a mental game refers to the undeniable truth that your external financial reality directly reflects your internal mental state. The beliefs, thoughts, and emotions you carry around money dictate how you handle, attract, and even repel it. People who are wealthy and stay wealthy have mastered this game by aligning their mindset with abundance. Those who struggle with money often haven't yet recognized the invisible barriers that exist in their own minds—barriers that block the flow of wealth into their lives.

This isn't just about positive thinking or wishful dreaming. It's about understanding the relationship between your unconscious beliefs, your conscious thoughts, and the actions you take or don't take in response to them. In other words, mastering the money game requires mastering your mind.

Unveiling the True Path to Financial Freedom

Many people who seek financial freedom focus primarily on external factors: how much money they earn, what they can do to save more, invest better, or manage their finances. While these things are undeniably important, they are only the surface layer of wealth creation. True, lasting financial freedom doesn't come from how much you earn—it comes from how you think about money and how aligned your mindset is with your financial goals.

Imagine for a moment that you have a garden. The money you want to grow is like a plant in that garden. You can give it water, sunshine, and fertilizer, and it may grow for a time, but if the soil is full of weeds, pests, or toxins, that plant will struggle. It might wither and die, no matter how much you nurture it. Your mind is like the soil in which your financial reality grows. Your wealth will struggle to flourish if it's filled with limiting beliefs, fear, and doubt.

This book is your guide to transforming your mental soil, removing the weeds, and nourishing it with empowering beliefs and thoughts. We'll delve deep into the concepts of mental energy, reprogramming your subconscious and learning to direct your focus in ways that align with abundance. The goal isn't just to improve your financial situation temporarily but to awaken a mindset that continuously attracts and sustains wealth.

From Acquisition to Cultivation

So, what does it mean to cultivate a wealth-driven mindset? Many people view wealth as something to be acquired—like a prize to be won. They chase money, believing that once they have enough, they'll finally feel free. But this approach often leads to burnout, frustration, and the realization that "enough" is always out of reach.

Embracing a wealth-driven mindset is like tending to a garden. It's not about chasing money but about nurturing the internal conditions that naturally attract it. When you shift your focus from acquisition to cultivation, you stop thinking of money as something external that you must get and start recognizing that it's a byproduct of who you are and how you think. Wealth becomes a reflection of your internal abundance. This doesn't mean that effort and action are unnecessary. They're crucial. However, the actions you take when you operate from a place of internal wealth are far more effective than those driven by a scarcity mindset.

You'll find that when your mind is aligned with abundance, the opportunities, people, and resources you need to build wealth appear almost effortlessly.

The Key to Sustainable Financial Freedom

Mindset is the key to sustainable financial freedom because it's the only thing you can truly control in an unpredictable world. Markets fluctuate, industries change, and economies rise and fall. But your mindset—how you perceive, respond to, and create in the face of these changes—determines whether you will thrive or struggle.

Consider for a moment the stories of self-made millionaires who lose everything only to rebuild their fortunes within a few years. What sets them apart from those who never recover from financial loss? It's not luck. It's not access to better resources. It's their mindset. These individuals have cultivated an internal wealth consciousness that allows them to bounce back, adapt, and seize opportunities in any situation. They understand that wealth is not something they own—it's something they embody.

The same is true for those who seem to win large sums of money or stumble upon sudden financial success, only to lose it just as quickly. Without the right mindset, sudden financial gain is often fleeting. This is why many lottery winners find themselves broke just a few years after winning. Their external circumstances changed, but their internal mindset around money remained the same, filled with scarcity, fear, or limiting beliefs that sabotaged their newfound wealth.

Sustainable financial freedom isn't about quick wins. It's about cultivating the proper mental habits and beliefs that support long-term wealth. This is the difference between fleeting success and lasting prosperity.

What You'll Learn in This Book

Throughout the chapters, we will explore wealth's mental and emotional aspects in a way that goes beyond traditional financial advice. We'll talk about money as energy, how to overcome the limiting beliefs that block you from wealth, and how to reprogram your subconscious mind for financial success. We'll explore the neuroscience of wealth, the power of focus, and the importance of emotional mastery in creating lasting abundance.

You'll learn how to harness the mental tools used by some of the wealthiest individuals in the world to attract, build, and sustain their fortunes. More importantly, you'll learn how to apply these tools in your life—no matter where you are financially.

The goal of this book is simple: to awaken your money mindset. By the time you've finished, you'll have a clearer understanding of your relationship with money and a new, empowered approach to wealth creation. You'll have the tools, techniques, and insights necessary to align your mind with abundance and create your desired financial reality.

Remember, financial freedom isn't just about what's in your bank account. It's about the state of your mind. When your mindset is awakened, money will naturally flow into your life. Wealth will no longer be something you chase—it will be something you attract.

So, as we begin this journey together, I encourage you to keep an open mind and be ready to challenge some of your beliefs about money. Awakening your money mindset may not always be easy, but it will be transformative. Are you ready to take the next step toward true financial freedom? Let's get started.

CHAPTER 1

The Awakening: Recognizing Money as Energy

As dawn breaks, the horizon is painted in vibrant hues of gold and lavender. It's as if the universe reminds us of the abundance surrounding us, the quiet but ever-present flow of energy beyond our eyes. At this moment, standing before the world's vastness, we are invited to awaken to the realization that **money, too, is energy**. This dynamic, vibrating force responds to the beliefs and emotions we carry within us.

Money is often considered concrete, tangible—coins, bills, numbers on a screen. But what if I told you that money is more than just paper and metal, more than numbers in your bank account? What if I told you that money, at its core, is a reflection of the energy you send out into the world?

Let's start with an image: picture a stream flowing effortlessly through a forest, glistening in the sunlight. The stream has no concept of lack or struggle. It flows because that is its nature. This is how money can flow into your life when you align your mindset with the truth of abundance. **Money is the stream**, an ever-flowing resource, and your beliefs and emotions are the banks guiding its course.

Money as Energy: More Than a Transaction

It's easy to see money as purely transactional: you exchange it for goods and services, pay bills, earn a paycheck, and so on. But this view is limited. To fully awaken to the power of financial freedom, we must begin to understand that **money is energy**, responding to the vibrations we emit.

Every thought, feeling, and belief you hold about money creates a frequency. This frequency sends out signals to the universe, telling it how to respond to you. Do you constantly worry about not having enough? That worry creates a low-frequency vibration, drawing in more circumstances that align with scarcity. On the other hand, when you feel gratitude, even for the slightest financial wins, you create a high-frequency vibration that attracts more abundance into your life.

Money is sensitive to these emotional and mental frequencies. Imagine money as a mirror. Whatever beliefs you hold up to in that mirror will be reflected in your financial reality. If you believe money is hard to come by, that's precisely what you'll experience. That will become your truth if you believe money flows easily and abundantly.

Emotional Frequencies: How They Shape Your Financial Reality

The frequencies we emit come from deeply rooted beliefs, often unconscious ones. As children, we absorb messages about money from our parents, our environment, and society. These early messages become the stories we tell ourselves about money as adults, shaping our relationship with it.

Let's pause and visualize something. Imagine you're in a grand library filled with towering bookshelves that stretch beyond sight. Each shelf is lined with leather-bound books, and inside each book is a story—Your **money story**. These stories contain the beliefs you've been telling yourself about money for years, whether you realize it or not.

Some of these stories are positive: "Money always finds its way to me" and "I am worthy of financial success." But many of these stories are limiting: "I'll never have enough," "Money is for other people, not me," and "I have to work hard and struggle to make ends meet."

These negative money stories create blockages in your energetic field, preventing money from flowing freely to you. The good news is that you have the power to rewrite these stories to clear the energetic clutter that holds you back. But first, you must become aware of them.

Recognizing Your Money Stories

Take a moment to reflect on your current financial situation. What words would you use to describe it? **Abundant? Stressful? Stable?** Now, dig a little deeper. What beliefs do you hold about money that might be contributing to this reality? Are they positive or negative?

Recognizing your money stories is the first step toward awakening your financial potential. Just as the subconscious mind controls much of our behavior without conscious awareness, these money stories operate beneath the surface, influencing how you relate to money daily.

Perhaps you grew up in a household where money was always a source of stress. Your parents might have argued about bills or instilled in you a belief that money was scarce. Now, as an adult, you might find yourself living out that same story, constantly feeling as though there's never enough, even when your bank account tells a different story. These early experiences leave energetic imprints that, if left unchecked, continue to play out in your financial reality.

But the moment you shine a light on these stories, you begin the transformation process. Imagine your negative money stories as shadows hiding in the corners of your mind. Once you illuminate them, they lose their power over you.

Shifting Your Beliefs: From Scarcity to Abundance

Once you've identified the stories you've been telling yourself, the next step is to **rewrite them**. This is where the magic of mindset comes into play. You change the energetic frequency you emit by consciously shifting your beliefs from scarcity to abundance. And as you shift your frequency, your financial reality will also begin to shift.

Picture a garden. If you plant seeds of scarcity—fear, doubt, and worry—your garden will struggle to grow. But if you plant seeds of abundance—gratitude, trust, and openness—you will cultivate a flourishing garden of prosperity. The mind works in much the same way. Whatever beliefs you plant in the fertile soil of your subconscious will take root and shape your financial reality.

To shift from a scarcity mindset to an abundance mindset, start by reframing your thoughts. Instead of saying, "I'll never have enough money," shift to, "Money is always available to me." Instead of focusing on debt, focus on the opportunities that allow you to increase your income. These simple shifts may feel awkward initially, but over time, they will rewire your brain and change the frequency you send out into the universe.

Your Money Mirrors Your Inner World

Imagine yourself standing in front of a mirror. In this mirror, you don't just see your physical reflection—you see the energy you emit. **Money is that mirror.** It reflects to you the beliefs and feelings you hold about it.

If your financial situation isn't where you'd like it to be, ask yourself: What is this mirror trying to show me? Are lingering beliefs of unworthiness, scarcity, or fear blocking the flow of abundance into your life?

The good news is that just as a mirror reflects what it sees, it can change when the person standing before it changes. As you shift your internal world—your beliefs, thoughts, and emotions—you'll begin to see a new reflection in the mirror of money. You'll see more opportunities, ease, and abundance flowing into your life.

The Power of Affirmations: Reprogramming Your Money Mindset

One of the most effective tools for shifting your money mindset is **affirmations**. Affirmations are positive statements that help reprogram your subconscious mind, aligning it with the energy of abundance.

Here are a few powerful money affirmations to incorporate into your daily routine:

- "I am open and receptive to all the wealth life offers me."
- "Money flows to me easily, frequently, and abundantly."
- "I am worthy of financial freedom and unlimited wealth."

- "Every dollar I spend comes back to me multiplied."

By repeating these affirmations daily, you begin to rewrite the stories you've been telling yourself about money. You shift your frequency, and as you do, money begins to respond to your new energetic state.

Practical Steps for Realigning Your Money Energy

While mindset is crucial, practical action is equally important. The universe rewards actions that are aligned with your new beliefs. Here are some steps you can take to begin realigning your money energy with abundance:

1. **Gratitude Journal**: Keep a daily journal in which you write down five things you are grateful for, especially related to money. This will shift your focus from lack to abundance.
2. **Spend Mindfully**: Treat every financial transaction as an energy flow, no matter how small. When you pay a bill, imagine sending positive energy into the world, trusting it will return to you tenfold.
3. **Invest in Yourself**: Whether it's education, personal development, or simply taking care of your health, investing in yourself is one of the most powerful ways to signal to the universe that you are worthy of abundance.
4. **Surround Yourself with Abundance**: Declutter your environment of things that no longer serve you. Create a space that reflects abundance, and you will attract more of it into your life.

Your Money Mindset Awakening

As we conclude this chapter, I invite you to reflect on the idea that **money is not something you must chase or struggle to obtain**. Instead, it is an energy that flows into your life when you align your beliefs and actions with abundance.

By recognizing money as energy and becoming aware of the stories you've been telling yourself, you have taken the first step toward financial freedom. The awakening has begun.

Real-Life Examples: How Beliefs Shape Financial Reality

To truly grasp the concept of money as energy, one needs to look at real-life examples. Consider two individuals: Sarah and James. Both earn a similar income, but their financial situations couldn't be more different.

Sarah constantly finds herself living paycheck to paycheck. No matter how much she earns, she always seems to be short on cash, scrambling to cover her bills by the end of the month. Deep down, Sarah believes that money is hard to come by and that she's not the kind of person meant to be wealthy. She worries about unexpected expenses and lives with the constant fear that one day, her financial situation will collapse entirely.

James, on the other hand, leads a different financial life. He has built up savings, invests regularly, and always seems to have money for what he wants.

James earns roughly the same amount as Sarah, but his mindset is fundamentally different. He believes that money flows easily into his life, and even when unexpected costs arise, he trusts that the universe will provide.

The difference between Sarah and James lies not in their income or job security but in the stories they've been telling themselves about money. Sarah's beliefs are rooted in scarcity, and as a result, her financial energy is blocked. James, however, operates from a mindset of abundance. His belief that money flows freely to him and that creates the conditions for that reality to manifest

Conclusion: The Dawn of Your Financial Awakening

Imagine standing at the edge of a vast ocean at sunrise. As the golden light spreads across the horizon, it touches the water's surface, transforming it into shimmering waves of possibility. In this metaphor, the ocean represents the limitless potential of financial abundance, and the sunlight is your awakened mindset, casting its glow over everything it touches.

This is your awakening—the moment when you realize that money is not a mysterious force you must chase or control. It is a wave of energy ready to flow into your life when you align your beliefs and actions with its natural current. Like the ocean tide, it ebbs and flows, responding to the moon-like pull of your inner world.

Your thoughts and beliefs are the wind that guides the sails of your financial ship. If your mind is clouded with doubt, fear, or unworthiness, the winds will be turbulent, and your journey toward financial freedom will feel slow and difficult. But when you fill your sails with belief in abundance, trust, and gratitude, your ship glides effortlessly across the waters, guided by a steady breeze toward the shores of wealth and opportunity.

Remember, **money is the mirror** of your internal world. Whatever you believe, whatever stories you hold onto will reflect in your financial reality. When you change the reflection inside the mirror and clear away the fog of scarcity, you see a new image: one of prosperity, ease, and endless possibility.

Just as a gardener plant seeds with the expectation that they will grow, so too can you plant the seeds of abundance in your mind. With time, attention, and care, these seeds will sprout into the financial success you've always desired. **Your mind is the soil** where these seeds take root, and the energy of money is the sunlight that helps them flourish.

Final Thoughts: Awakening to Abundance

As we close this chapter, remember that your journey toward financial freedom is like a beautiful flower unfolding. At first, the bud is closed, tight with potential, but not yet in full bloom. With each new belief, thought, and step you take, the petals begin to open, revealing the vibrant, abundant life that was always within you.

You are the gardener, the sailor, the artist of your financial reality. You can change your mindset, rewrite your money stories, and tune into the energy of abundance.

The moment you awaken to this truth, you step into a new world—one where money is no longer a source of stress or fear but a powerful, flowing energy that supports your highest vision of life.

So, stand at the edge of that vast ocean. Feel the breeze on your face and the warmth of the rising sun. The world of financial freedom is before you, waiting for you to claim it. With your awakened mindset and newfound understanding, you are ready to embark on your life's most exciting and transformative journey.

In the next chapter, we'll look into identifying and how to overcome limiting beliefs.

CHAPTER 2

Mental Blocks Identifying and Overcoming Limiting Beliefs

Imagine walking through a lush, vibrant forest, with trees towering above and the path beneath your feet soft and inviting. Suddenly, you come across a large stone wall blocking your way. You can hear the sound of a waterfall just beyond it—the flow of abundance—but you can't seem to get past this wall. Standing firm and immovable, that wall represents **your limiting beliefs about money**.

To reach the waterfall, the symbol of financial freedom, you must first confront and dismantle this wall. These mental blocks, often hidden deep within, form the boundaries of your current financial reality. Without realizing it, many of us have constructed these walls over the years, brick by brick, through cultural, familial, and societal conditioning. But the good news is that these walls aren't permanent. Just as they were built, they can be taken down.

The Nature of Limiting Beliefs

Let's begin by understanding what **limiting beliefs** are. Essentially, they are thoughts or assumptions that act as barriers between you and your potential for wealth and abundance. These beliefs often exist in our subconscious, silently guiding our actions and decisions, and are typically formed during childhood. Once you recognize them, you'll notice how much control they have over your financial reality.

Limiting beliefs are like **shadows cast by the past**, lingering long after the circumstances that created them have disappeared. They're the unspoken rules we internalize based on the environment in which we were raised and our experiences. When it comes to money, these beliefs tend to be passed down through generations, reinforced by societal narratives and personal experiences.

Let's look at some common examples of limiting beliefs about money:

- "Money is the root of all evil."
- "Rich people are greedy."
- "I'm just not good with money."
- "I have to work hard for money."
- "There's never enough to go around."
- "I'm not the kind of person who can be wealthy."

These beliefs may feel familiar, but they are **false narratives** that distort your understanding of what's possible.

Cultural, Familial, and Societal Conditioning Around Money

Limiting beliefs are often handed down to us by the world around us, mainly through cultural, familial, and societal conditioning. It's as though these beliefs are **inherited scripts**, silently written into our subconscious minds before we even have the chance to question them.

Family: The Seedbed of Beliefs

Whether they were conscious of it or not, your family played a significant role in shaping your relationship with money. Think back to your childhood. What messages did you hear about money growing up? Were your parents stressed about finances? Did they say things like, "We can't afford that," or, "You have to save every penny because you never know what could happen?"

Families often perpetuate cycles of financial struggle, not because they intend to, but because they're passing down beliefs that were taught to them. It's like an **old, worn-out blueprint**—a set of instructions that no longer serves the modern world but continues to shape our financial behavior. If your family saw money as something scarce, it's likely you absorbed that belief as well, and without realizing it, you may still be operating from that place of scarcity.

Culture: The Larger Framework

Cultural beliefs about money are powerful. In some cultures, there is a deep-rooted suspicion of wealth, with phrases like, "Money can't buy happiness" or "The rich get richer, and the poor get poorer," being passed around as universal truths. In others, success and wealth are so idealized that people are driven to exhaustion trying to achieve them, believing their worth is tied to their financial success.

Whatever the cultural narrative, it influences how we view money, whether consciously or not. Take a moment to reflect on the messages that your culture sends about wealth. Are those messages empowering or limiting? Are they encouraging you to pursue abundance or creating guilt and fear around it?

Society: The External Pressure

Society at large has a way of reinforcing limiting beliefs about money, particularly through media, advertising, and social norms. From a young age, we are bombarded with mixed messages. We are told to pursue wealth and success, but at the same time, we see headlines criticizing the wealthy or hear stories of corruption tied to money. This creates an internal conflict where we want to achieve financial freedom, but we feel hesitant about the idea of wealth itself.

Consider the classic narrative of the **self-made millionaire**—someone who worked tirelessly, sacrificed personal happiness, and eventually "made it." While this story can be inspiring, it also subtly reinforces the belief that wealth comes only through struggle and that success requires extreme hardship.

Identifying Your Money Blocks

The key to overcoming limiting beliefs is to **recognize** them. Until you bring these beliefs to the surface, they will continue to operate in the background, shaping your financial reality. This recognition process is much like walking into a dark room with a flashlight.

Once you shine the light on the hidden corners of your mind, you can see the obstacles holding you back.

Let's look at a few tools and exercises to help you identify your money blocks:

1. The Money Autobiography

Writing your money autobiography is a powerful way to uncover your limiting beliefs. This involves reflecting on your financial life from childhood to today and exploring the essential experiences shaping your relationship with money. As you write, ask yourself the following questions:

- What was my first memory of money?
- How did my parents handle money, and what did they teach me about it?
- What financial struggles or successes did I witness growing up?
- How do I feel about money now? Is it a source of stress or empowerment?

By answering these questions, you'll begin to see patterns and beliefs that may have been guiding your financial behavior for years.

2. The Money Belief Inventory

Another exercise is the **Money Belief Inventory**, where you list all your beliefs about money. Write down every thought that comes to mind without filtering yourself. These could be beliefs like, "I'm not good with money," "I'll never get out of debt," or "I always have enough." Once you've listed these beliefs, separate them into two categories: **empowering** and **limiting**.

This exercise will help you see which beliefs are working for you and which are working against you. You'll want to focus on reframing the limiting beliefs.

Reframing Limiting Beliefs: Breaking Down the Wall

Once you've identified your limiting beliefs, the next step is to **reframe** them into empowering perspectives. Think of this process as **demolishing the stone wall** you encountered in the forest earlier. Each limiting belief is like a brick in that wall, and by reframing these beliefs, you begin to take the wall apart, brick by brick, until the path to abundance is clear.

1. Challenge the Belief

The first step in reframing a limiting belief is to **challenge its validity**. Ask yourself: Is this belief true? For example, if you believe, "I have to work really hard to make money," ask yourself if that's universally true. Are there people who earn money with ease and joy?

The answer is likely yes, which means the belief you've been holding onto is not a fixed reality—it's just a perspective.

By challenging your beliefs, you open up the possibility that they might not be as solid as you once thought.

2. Replace the Limiting Belief

Once you've challenged the limiting belief, replace it with a new, empowering one. For instance, instead of saying, "I'm just not good with money," reframe it to, "I am learning to master money and create wealth." This simple shift transforms a fixed mindset into a **growth mindset**, where you see your relationship with money as something you can change and improve over time.

Here are a few examples of reframed beliefs:

- Limiting: "Money is the root of all evil." Reframed: "Money is a tool that allows me to create positive change in the world."
- Limiting: "I'm not the kind of person who can be wealthy." Reframed: "I am worthy of financial abundance, and it is available to me."
- Limiting: "There's never enough to go around." Reframed: "The universe is abundant, and there is more than enough for everyone."

3. Anchor the New Belief

Once you've replaced the limiting belief, it's important to anchor the new belief in your mind. This can be done through daily affirmations, visualizations, or simply repeating the new belief whenever you catch yourself slipping back into old thought patterns. The more you reinforce the new belief, the stronger it becomes.

Visualization: Clearing the Path to Abundance

To help solidify these new beliefs, let's try a powerful visualization exercise.

Close your eyes and imagine yourself standing in a dense forest. The wall of limiting beliefs looms before you, blocking your path. Now, see yourself holding a powerful tool—a sledgehammer of clarity, awareness, and self-belief. You swing the hammer individually, shattering each brick of doubt, fear, and insecurity. With each swing, you feel lighter, stronger, more empowered.

As the wall crumbles, a bright, open path is revealed. The sunlight floods in, illuminating your way forward. Feel the warmth of the light on your skin, the sense of openness and freedom. This is the path to your abundance—clear, unobstructed, and ready to walk confidently.

Now, take a step forward. Each step you take is filled with the knowledge that you deserve abundance and are fully capable of achieving it. The forest around you represents life's challenges, but the path you've cleared remains open, guiding you toward your goals.

Stay here momentarily, basking in this sense of possibility and empowerment. When you're ready, slowly open your eyes and carry this feeling of clarity and strength with you.

Real-Life Application: Putting the Tools to Use

At this point, you've learned about the nature of limiting beliefs, identified some of your own, and discovered how to challenge and reframe them. Now, it's time to put these tools into action. Like a gardener preparing the soil before planting seeds, you've cleared the mental blocks that once stood in the way of abundance. Now, you're ready to cultivate new, empowering beliefs that will shape your financial future.

But how do you maintain this new mindset when life throws challenges your way? How do you stay aligned with abundance when unexpected expenses arise or when old patterns try to resurface?

Here are some practical steps you can take to reinforce the work you've done so far:

1. Daily Mindset Practice

Just as you would exercise regularly to keep your body healthy, your money mindset requires daily attention to stay strong. Set aside a few minutes each day to focus on your financial well-being. This could involve repeating affirmations, journaling about your money goals, or visualizing the abundance you want to create.

For example, each morning, you might say, "I am worthy of wealth, and money flows to me easily and frequently." By doing this consistently, you're rewiring your subconscious mind to align with abundance rather than scarcity.

2. Create a Vision Board

A powerful way to keep your focus on abundance is to create a **vision board** that represents your financial goals and dreams. Gather images, words, and symbols that reflect the kind of life you want to live. Perhaps it's a picture of the dream house you want to buy, a vacation you've always wanted to take, or words like "freedom" and "wealth" that resonate with your new beliefs.

Hang the vision board somewhere you can see it every day. Each time you look at it, remind yourself that you are actively creating the life reflected on that board, brick by brick, belief by belief.

3. Track Your Progress

Keep a journal to document your financial progress. Note the changes in your mindset, the opportunities that come your way, and the small (or big) financial wins you experience. Tracking your progress keeps you motivated and reminds you of the power of your new beliefs.

As time goes on, you'll start to see how these small shifts in your thinking lead to larger, tangible changes in your financial reality.

4. Surround Yourself with Abundance

One often overlooked aspect of creating wealth is the **energy** of your environment. If you surround yourself with scarcity—clutter, debt, or people who reinforce negative beliefs about money—it will be much harder to maintain an abundance mindset.

Start by decluttering your physical space. Clear out anything that feels like it's weighing you down or representing scarcity. Then, take a look at the people in your life. Do they support your financial growth, or do they reinforce limiting beliefs? Surround yourself with people who uplift you, encourage you, and share a positive relationship with money.

This doesn't mean you need to cut people out of your life, but it does mean setting boundaries around conversations about money. When you hear someone complaining about their finances or talking about money negatively, use it to reflect on your beliefs and how far you've come.

Reclaiming Your Financial Power: The Butterfly Effect

Imagine for a moment that you're watching a butterfly emerge from its chrysalis. It's a delicate, almost miraculous process as the butterfly carefully breaks free from its former shell. In this metaphor, **you are the butterfly**, and the limiting beliefs you've carried are the chrysalis—something that once served a purpose but is now holding you back from the freedom and flight that await you.

Breaking free of your old financial mindset might initially feel slow and uncertain, just like the butterfly's emergence. But each step you take toward abundance, each limiting belief you replace, is a flap of your wings. And just as the butterfly's wings can create ripples in the air, your newfound beliefs can create ripples in your financial life.

This process of financial transformation may not always be dramatic or instantaneous. But over time, small shifts in your mindset—the small flaps of your wings—create a butterfly effect that changes your entire financial landscape. Opportunities that once seemed out of reach become available to you, and money that once felt elusive begins to flow naturally into your life.

This is the power of aligning your beliefs with abundance. It's not about sudden windfalls or overnight success. It's about consistent, intentional change transforming your relationship with money and your entire life.

Final Thoughts: Your Path Forward

As we conclude this chapter, it's important to remember that the journey toward financial freedom isn't about perfection. You may encounter setbacks, and old limiting beliefs may occasionally resurface. But the difference now is that you are aware. You have the tools to recognize when a limiting belief is holding you back, and you have the power to reframe it.

Think of your financial journey as a path through a forest. At first, the way forward might seem unclear, with overgrown branches and hidden obstacles. But the path becomes more evident with each step you take—each belief you identify, challenge, and reframe. The more you walk this path, the easier it becomes, until one day, you find yourself standing in a wide-open clearing, bathed in sunlight. This clearing represents your financial freedom—a place where abundance flows naturally, where you feel empowered and in control of your financial destiny.

Remember, this journey isn't linear. With each step, there will be twists and turns, but you're getting closer to your desired financial life. Trust yourself, trust the process, and know that every effort you put into reshaping your mindset brings you closer to lasting abundance.

The next chapter will delve deeper into the subconscious mind and explore powerful reprogramming techniques for lasting wealth. By harnessing the power of your inner beliefs, you will be well on your way to creating the financial life you've always dreamed of.

CHAPTER 3

The Subconscious Blueprint Reprogramming for Wealth
Understanding the Subconscious Mind as the Foundation for Wealth Creation

Wealth creation begins far before any conscious action—before the business plans, the financial decisions, or even the dreams of abundance. It starts in the mind, specifically in the subconscious. Think of your subconscious mind as the soil where your financial habits, beliefs, and outcomes take root. If the soil is rich and fertile, your seeds of abundance can grow into wealth and prosperity. However, even the best financial strategies will struggle to take hold if the soil is full of limiting beliefs, negative attitudes, and scarcity mindsets.

The subconscious mind is mighty, operating about 95% of our lives on autopilot. This part of the mind holds deeply ingrained beliefs, behaviors, and emotional patterns that dictate how we respond to life's circumstances—including our relationship with money. While we may consciously desire financial success, our subconscious mind often harbors conflicting programs, holding us back from reaching our full potential.

To fully understand wealth creation, it's essential to recognize that the subconscious mind controls how you think, feel, and act about money. These patterns can either support or sabotage your efforts to build wealth. Therefore, reprogramming the subconscious mind is critical if you want to align your internal beliefs with your financial goals.

Early Programming: How Life Experiences Shape Financial Habits

From a very young age, we are shaped by our environment. Our beliefs and attitudes about money are often inherited from our parents, caregivers, or influential figures in our lives. These experiences form the mental blueprint that governs our relationship with wealth.

For instance, if you grew up hearing phrases like "Money doesn't grow on trees" or "We can't afford that," your subconscious mind internalizes the belief that money is scarce and hard to come by. Alternatively, if you witnessed financial abundance and were taught that wealth was attainable and abundant, your subconscious blueprint may support the pursuit of economic success more naturally.

These early experiences often manifest in adult life as financial habits and patterns. Do you constantly worry about money, even when there's no immediate financial threat? Or perhaps you sabotage financial opportunities, feeling like you're not deserving of abundance. These are indicators that your subconscious programming around wealth is working against you. The good news is that these patterns can be changed. Your past experiences do not bind you. You can create new financial habits that align with wealth and prosperity by identifying limiting beliefs and reprogramming your subconscious mind.

Practical Techniques for Rewiring the Subconscious Mind

The power to reprogram your subconscious mind lies in repetition and emotion. The subconscious is most responsive to consistent, emotionally charged experiences. This means that by regularly engaging in practices promoting abundance and positive financial beliefs, you can rewrite the limiting scripts holding you back.

Let's explore some practical techniques you can use to rewire your subconscious mind for wealth.

1. Affirmations

Affirmations are positive, present-tense statements that help recondition the subconscious mind. They work by replacing negative, self-limiting beliefs with empowering ones. When repeated consistently and with emotion, affirmations convey to your subconscious mind that new, positive patterns are forming.

To create effective wealth-building affirmations, focus on statements that reflect the reality you want to create. For example:

- "I am worthy of financial abundance."
- "Money flows to me easily and effortlessly."
- "I am a magnet for prosperity and wealth."
- "I make wise financial decisions that lead to abundance."

To maximize the power of affirmations, repeat them daily, preferably in the morning or before bed when the subconscious mind is most receptive. You can say them aloud, write them down, or even listen to them in audio form.

2. Visualization

Visualization is another powerful technique for reprogramming your subconscious. When you visualize your financial goals vividly and with emotion, you send a clear signal to your subconscious that this is your desired reality. The subconscious mind doesn't differentiate between real and imagined experiences; it will align your thoughts, behaviors, and actions to make that vision a reality.

Here's a step-by-step guide to creating a powerful wealth visualization:

1. **Find a Quiet Space**: Sit comfortably, close your eyes, and relax.
2. **Create a Clear Picture**: Imagine yourself living your ideal financial life. See yourself paying off debts, growing your savings, investing, and enjoying financial freedom. Make this vision as detailed as possible.
3. **Engage Your Emotions**: Feel the emotions associated with this vision. Experience the joy, freedom, and relief that come with financial abundance.
4. **Repetition is Key**: Practice this visualization daily to reinforce the new belief patterns in your subconscious mind.

By consistently visualizing your financial goals, you're training your subconscious to accept these new possibilities as truth.

3. Self-Hypnosis

Self-hypnosis is a deeper way of accessing the subconscious mind and reprogramming it for success. Hypnosis places the brain in a relaxed, focused state known as the theta brainwave, where the subconscious is most malleable.

You can perform self-hypnosis by following these steps:

1. **Relax**: Find a quiet place and sit or lie down comfortably. Close your eyes and take deep, calming breaths.

2. **Focus Your Mind**: Slowly count from 10 to 1, relaxing more profound with each number. As you count, focus on releasing tension from your body.

3. **Introduce New Beliefs**: In this relaxed state, repeat your affirmations or visualize your financial goals. Imagine wealth flowing to you and focus on the feelings of abundance.

4. **Reinforce the Message**: Stay relaxed for 10-20 minutes, continuing to reinforce positive financial beliefs.

5. **Awaken Slowly**: Gently count up from 1 to 5 and open your eyes, feeling refreshed and empowered.

By regularly practicing self-hypnosis, you can bypass the conscious mind's resistance and speak directly to the subconscious, where deep transformation occurs.

Exercises for Reprogramming the Subconscious

To help solidify these techniques, let's explore some practical exercises you can do to reprogram your subconscious mind for wealth.

Exercise 1: Identify Limiting Beliefs

The first step to reprogramming the subconscious is identifying the limiting beliefs that are currently in place. Take some time to reflect on your financial habits and attitudes. Ask yourself the following questions:

- What beliefs about money did I learn growing up?
- Do I feel that I deserve to be wealthy? Why or why not?
- What negative thoughts do I have when I think about wealth or rich people?
- Do I have fears about losing money or being unable to sustain wealth?

Write down any limiting beliefs that surface. Once you've identified them, you can begin the process of reprogramming.

Exercise 2: Rewrite Your Money Story

After identifying your limiting beliefs, it's time to rewrite your money story. This is where you get to change the narrative around wealth in your life.

1. **Acknowledge the Old Story**: Write down your current story about money. For example, "I always struggle to make ends meet" or "I can never seem to save enough."
2. **Rewrite the New Story**: Now, take control of the narrative and rewrite it positively and empoweringly. For instance, "I am financially free, and money flows to me effortlessly," or "I have more than enough to meet my needs and save for the future."
3. **Live the New Story**: Read your new story aloud daily, ideally in front of a mirror. Feel the emotions as if this new story is already your reality. Over time, your subconscious will accept it as true.

Exercise 3: Future Self Meditation

This meditation is designed to connect you with your future self—the version of you that has already achieved financial abundance.

1. **Find a Quiet Space**: Sit comfortably, close your eyes, and take a few deep breaths.
2. **Visualize Your Future Self**: Imagine yourself 5 or 10 years in the future. See yourself living in abundance—what does your home look like? What is your financial situation? How do you feel knowing you've achieved wealth?

3. **Ask for Guidance**: Imagine conversing with your future self. Ask them for advice on how to achieve the level of financial success they have and listen closely to their wisdom.

4. **Embrace the Energy**: Feel the energy of your future self—confident, secure, and abundant. Carry this energy with you as you move through your daily life.

By regularly practicing this meditation, you'll start aligning your current self with the successful, wealthy version of yourself.

Aligning the Subconscious with Abundance

Reprogramming the subconscious mind for wealth is an ongoing process. As you continue to use affirmations, visualization, self-hypnosis, and meditation, you will gradually begin to see shifts in your beliefs and behaviors around money. You'll notice that you're no longer operating from a place of lack or fear but instead from a mindset of abundance, empowerment, and possibility.

The key to lasting change is consistency. Regularly practicing these techniques will train your subconscious to align with the vibration of abundance, allowing wealth and prosperity to flow naturally into your life. It may take time, but the rewards are worth the effort. Each time you engage in these practices, you create new neural pathways that support your financial success, replacing the old patterns of scarcity with ones rooted in abundance.

Remember, wealth starts within. When you change your internal beliefs and mindset, external results will follow. The subconscious mind is your most powerful ally in creating a life of abundance—learn to harness it, and the possibilities are limitless.

As you move forward, know that the work you've done so far—challenging limiting beliefs and consciously reprogramming your mind—has set the stage for an even more profound transformation. Now that you've begun to shift your internal world, it's time to explore the neuroscience behind these practices and understand how your brain can be trained for prosperity.

In the next chapter, we'll dive into the cutting-edge science of neuroplasticity and how thought patterns shape your financial reality. You'll discover how to leverage your brain's natural ability to change and learn specific techniques to rewire your brain for wealth, allowing you to think differently about money and act differently. This is where mindset meets science, and your journey toward financial freedom takes on a new level of depth and possibility.

CHAPTER 4

The Neuroscience of Wealth Training Your Brain for Prosperity

We often think of wealth as external money in the bank, investments, assets, or material possessions. Yet, neuroscience teaches us that wealth begins within the mind. In fact, the very patterns of thought we hold, the way our brains process information about money, and how we view opportunities play a profound role in determining our financial reality. Just as athletes train their bodies for peak physical performance, you can train your brain for economic success.

This chapter explores the fascinating field of neuroscience and how it impacts our ability to create wealth. From understanding brain plasticity to leveraging powerful tools like gratitude, you will learn how to rewire your mind for prosperity. The goal is to give you the science behind how the brain influences wealth and actionable techniques you can apply to recondition your thinking.

The Neuroscience of Wealth: How Your Brain Shapes Your Financial Reality

At its core, neuroscience is the study of the nervous system, including the brain. Recent advances in the field have revealed something remarkable: our brains are not fixed but malleable. This concept is called *neuroplasticity*, and it refers to the brain's ability to reorganize itself by forming new neural connections throughout life. What this means for wealth creation is profound: by changing the way you think, you can change how your brain operates, thus influencing your ability to perceive and seize financial opportunities.

The brain operates primarily on patterns. Wealth patterns are often established early in life. For example, if you grew up in an environment where money was scarce, your brain may be conditioned to operate from a place of fear, avoidance, or scarcity. On the other hand, if you were exposed to positive financial habits, your brain is likely wired to approach money with confidence and abundance.

Here's the critical point: no matter what your early experiences with money were, you can change these patterns. The brain, through neuroplasticity, can be rewired to think differently about wealth. This ability to reshape thought patterns is not just theoretical—neuroscience research confirms that with the right strategies, anyone can retrain their brain for financial success.

Neuroplasticity: Rewiring the Brain for Wealth

Neuroplasticity is the brain's remarkable ability to reorganize by forming new neural connections.

Every thought you think, every habit you cultivate, and every belief you reinforce strengthens specific neural pathways. Over time, these pathways become the default modes of thinking.

When it comes to wealth, many people are stuck in neural loops of scarcity. These loops are not just mental beliefs; they are ingrained neural patterns. The good news is that you can rewire these pathways, but doing so requires intentional effort.

Think of your brain as a dense forest. The more often you walk down a particular trail, the more defined and more accessible that path becomes. If your financial mindset has been dominated by scarcity, that trail is likely well-worn. But with consistent effort, you can carve out a new path leading to abundance and prosperity. At first, the new trail may be difficult to navigate, overgrown with old habits and limiting beliefs. But as you continue to walk this new path, it becomes easier to follow, and the old scarcity pathway begins to fade.

The Science of Thought Patterns and Money: Why We Tend to Default to Scarcity

Neuroscience research suggests that humans are wired for survival, not necessarily for abundance. The brain has a *negativity bias*, meaning it's more likely to focus on potential threats or losses rather than opportunities or gains. This bias stems from our evolutionary history, where being attuned to danger increases our chances of survival. However, this negativity bias can manifest in modern times as a scarcity mindset—constantly worrying about not having enough or losing what we already have.

Scarcity thinking activates the amygdala, the brain's fear center. When the amygdala is activated, it triggers the *fight or flight* response, diverting energy away from rational thinking in the prefrontal cortex, which is responsible for decision-making and planning. This explains why people often make poor financial decisions when operating from a place of fear. For example, you might avoid investing in opportunities that could grow your wealth because your brain is focused on the immediate risk of loss rather than the potential for long-term gain.

However, the more you train your brain to focus on abundance, the less reactive the amygdala becomes. Engaging in practices promoting an abundance mindset can reduce the brain's tendency to default to fear-based thinking.

From Scarcity to Abundance: Techniques to Rewire Your Brain

Shifting from a scarcity mindset to an abundance mindset requires deliberate practice. Here are a few neuroscience-backed techniques to help you rewire your brain for prosperity:

1. Visualization: Creating Mental Blueprints for Wealth

Visualization is not just a motivational tool; it's a powerful way to activate the brain's neural networks. When you visualize yourself achieving financial success, you engage the same neural circuits that would be active if you were experiencing that success in real life.

One of the reasons visualization works is due to the brain's *mirror neuron system*. Mirror neurons fire when you perform an action and when you observe someone else performing that action. This means that when you vividly imagine yourself achieving a financial goal, your brain processes it as if it's already happening. This primes your brain to take actions that align with your vision.

To practice visualization effectively, find a quiet place and close your eyes. Picture yourself in a future where your financial goals have been achieved. Imagine the sights, sounds, and feelings associated with this success. Be as detailed as possible. The more sensory detail you include, the more powerful the visualization becomes. Over time, this practice strengthens the neural pathways associated with abundance and wealth, making recognizing and acting on opportunities easier.

2. Gratitude: Rewiring the Brain to Focus on Opportunity

Gratitude is often seen as a feel-good practice, but its benefits extend far beyond emotion. Neuroscientific research shows that practicing gratitude regularly can actually rewire the brain. Brain imaging studies have found that gratitude activates the brain's reward centers, including the ventromedial prefrontal cortex, which is associated with decision-making and rewards.

When you focus on what you're grateful for, the brain releases dopamine and serotonin, two neurotransmitters that enhance mood and make you feel good. More importantly, gratitude reduces activity in the amygdala, lowering fear and anxiety. This shift allows your brain to focus on opportunities rather than threats.

Gratitude also improves the brain's ability to recognize patterns of abundance. By acknowledging what you already have, you train your brain to notice more opportunities for growth and success. Essentially, gratitude helps you build a mental framework of abundance, making attracting wealth into your life easier.

Exercise: Each day, write down three things you are grateful for, especially in the realm of finances. They don't have to be tremendous accomplishments—perhaps you're grateful for having enough to pay your bills or for the opportunity to learn new financial strategies. Over time, this practice will help recondition your brain to focus on abundance.

3. Cognitive Reappraisal: Changing Your Money Story

Cognitive reappraisal is a psychological technique for reframing negative or limiting thoughts into more positive, empowering ones. It's essentially the act of changing one's inner dialogue. Neuroscientifically, cognitive reappraisal activates the prefrontal cortex, helping one think more rationally and strategically.

For example, if you catch yourself thinking, "I'll never be able to get out of debt," cognitive reappraisal allows you to reframe that thought to something more empowering, like, "I'm taking steps each day to improve my financial situation." By consistently reframing limiting thoughts, you strengthen the neural pathways associated with positive, goal-oriented thinking.

Regarding brain structure, cognitive reappraisal strengthens the connections between the prefrontal cortex (responsible for rational thinking) and the amygdala (responsible for emotional responses). This connection helps reduce fear-based responses to financial challenges, allowing you to approach money decisions more calmly and confidently.

Exercise: Next time you encounter a financial challenge, pause and identify any limiting beliefs or negative thoughts that arise. Then, consciously reframe the thought into a more positive, solution-focused one.

4. Affirmations: Reprogramming the Subconscious

Affirmations are positive statements that, when repeated consistently, can reprogram your subconscious mind. Neuroscientifically, affirmations work by activating the brain's *reticular activating system* (RAS), a network of neurons that helps filter and prioritize information. When you focus on a particular affirmation, the RAS becomes attuned to that statement and starts to filter out information that contradicts it while highlighting information that supports it.

For example, if your affirmation is "I am worthy of financial success," your brain will start filtering information to reinforce this belief. Over time, affirmations can lead to lasting changes in how you perceive yourself and your ability to create wealth.

Exercise: Choose three affirmations related to wealth and repeat them out loud every morning and night. Some examples include: "Money flows easily to me," "I am financially abundant," and "Opportunities for wealth are all around me."

The Power of Consistency: How to Make These Practices Stick

Rewiring your brain for wealth is not a one-time event; it's a process that requires consistent effort. Neuroscience shows that repetition strengthens neural connections, making new thought patterns more automatic. The key to shifting from a scarcity mindset to an abundance mindset is regular practice—just like strengthening a muscle, your brain needs repeated training to solidify new habits.

Each time you practice visualization, gratitude, cognitive reappraisal, or affirmations, you reinforce the neural pathways that lead to an abundance mindset. Over time, these practices will shift your brain's default state from fear or scarcity to confidence and opportunity.

However, consistency can be challenging, especially when old habits or limiting beliefs resurface. Here are some ways to stay on track:

- **Create Rituals**: Incorporate these practices into your daily routine. For example, start each morning with a short gratitude exercise or end each day with a visualization of your financial goals. By anchoring these practices to specific times of day, you're more likely to stay consistent.

- **Track Your Progress**: Keep a journal to track your mental and financial progress. Reflect on how your mindset is shifting and note any small wins or opportunities that arise. This will keep you accountable and reinforce positive changes in your brain.
- **Be Patient with Yourself**: Changing thought patterns takes time. Neuroscience shows that it can take 21 to 66 days to form a new habit, depending on the individual and the habit being formed. Trust the process, and don't be discouraged by setbacks. Every time you engage in these practices, you are making progress, even if it doesn't feel immediate.

The Neuroscience of Abundance: How to Recognize and Seize Financial Opportunities

One of the most powerful outcomes of rewiring your brain for wealth is that it changes how you perceive the world around you. Once your brain begins operating from a place of abundance, you become more attuned to opportunities that may have previously gone unnoticed.

Here's why: The brain's *reticular activating system* (RAS) filters the overwhelming amount of information we encounter daily. It decides what gets our attention and what gets filtered out. When your brain is programmed for scarcity, the RAS focuses on threats or what you lack. But when you reprogram your mind for abundance, the RAS focuses on potential opportunities and resources that support your goals.

For instance, let's say you're looking to grow your income. Before rewiring your brain, you might not have noticed the freelance opportunities, investments, or partnerships that could have expanded your financial situation. However, with an abundance mindset, your brain is primed to recognize and act on these opportunities. Suddenly, things that once seemed invisible or out of reach come into focus.

This is why gratitude, visualization, and affirmations are so important—they continuously signal to your brain that abundance is possible, and opportunities are everywhere. Over time, you'll find that you're thinking differently about money and behaving differently. You'll take more risks, try new things, and embrace challenges with a mindset of growth rather than fear.

Gratitude: A Neuroscientific Shortcut to Success

Gratitude is one of the fastest ways to rewire your brain for abundance because it immediately shifts your focus from what's missing to what's already present. Neuroscientifically, gratitude has been shown to increase activity in the *medial prefrontal cortex*, an area of the brain associated with decision-making, empathy, and long-term planning. By regularly practicing gratitude, you're reshaping your brain to be more optimistic and open to financial growth.

Gratitude doesn't mean ignoring financial difficulties or pretending everything is perfect. Instead, it's about acknowledging the good in your life, no matter how small, and using that acknowledgment to build a foundation of abundance. The brain is a powerful pattern recognition machine, and the more you train it to recognize abundance, the more opportunities for wealth it will identify.

Exercise: Every night before bed, write down three things you're grateful for in your financial life, no matter how small. This could be anything from having a roof over your head to finding a great deal on groceries. Over time, this simple practice will rewire your brain to see more opportunities for financial growth and success.

How to Maintain an Abundance Mindset in a World of Scarcity

Adopting an abundance mindset is easy when things are going well, but what happens when you face financial stress, challenges, or even crises? Neuroscience shows that under stress, the brain reverts to old, ingrained patterns—often rooted in scarcity and fear. The amygdala, the part of the brain responsible for processing fear, can override the prefrontal cortex, which is responsible for rational thinking and decision-making.

To maintain an abundance mindset in difficult times, you must consciously activate the prefrontal cortex, which allows you to make decisions based on long-term goals rather than short-term fears. Here's how:

1. **Pause and Breathe**: When you feel overwhelmed by financial stress, take a moment to breathe deeply. This simple act calms the nervous system and reduces amygdala activity. In this calmer state, you'll be better able to access rational thought and make decisions from a place of abundance rather than fear.
2. **Reframe the Situation**: Cognitive reappraisal is a powerful tool here. When faced with a challenge, ask yourself how this situation might present an opportunity for growth. For example, if you experience a financial setback, you can reframe it as an opportunity to learn new financial strategies or reevaluate your spending habits.
3. **Return to Gratitude**: Even in challenging times, there is always something to be grateful for. By focusing on what you have rather than your lack, you shift your brain out of scarcity mode and back into abundance. Gratitude acts as a reset button for your brain, allowing you to approach problems more clearly and opportunistically.

The Future of Neuroscience and Wealth Creation

As neuroscience advances, we gain deeper insights into how the brain affects every aspect of our lives—including wealth. One exciting area of research is the role of *neurogenesis*, the process by which new neurons are formed in the brain. Scientists have discovered that neurogenesis doesn't stop after childhood; it continues into adulthood, particularly in the hippocampus, a brain region involved in memory and learning. This means that your brain can grow and change throughout your life, regardless of your age or financial history.

The implications for wealth creation are profound. With the right mental practices—such as those outlined in this chapter—you can grow new brain cells supporting abundance, creativity, and financial success. As you cultivate an abundance mindset, your brain becomes more adaptable, resilient, and attuned to opportunities.

The future of wealth lies not just in external factors like the stock market or real estate but in your brain's ability to adapt, learn, and grow. By continuing to engage in practices that support neuroplasticity, gratitude, and abundance, you are training your brain for lifelong prosperity.

Final Thoughts: Training Your Brain for Lifelong Prosperity

Your brain is your greatest asset in the journey toward financial success. By leveraging the principles of neuroscience, you can rewire your thought patterns, shift from scarcity to abundance, and open your mind to new opportunities for wealth.

The tools shared in this chapter—visualization, gratitude, cognitive reappraisal, and affirmations—are not just abstract concepts; they are proven methods to reshape your brain's wiring. With consistent practice, you will notice a transformation not only in your mindset but also in your financial reality.

Remember, the journey toward wealth is not just about accumulating money. It's about training your brain to see the world through the lens of abundance. It's about creating a mindset that attracts opportunities, overcomes challenges, and continuously seeks growth.

In the next chapter, we will explore practical financial strategies that align with your new, wealth-focused mindset, helping you turn your internal transformation into tangible financial success.

CHAPTER 5

The Power of Focus Directing Mental Energy Toward Wealth Creation

The ability to focus is one of the most underestimated tools in wealth creation. In an age filled with distractions, many people fail to realize that their greatest asset in achieving financial success is their ability to direct mental energy toward wealth-generating activities. Focus is not just about concentrating on a task; it's about aligning your thoughts, intentions, and actions with your financial goals. When you learn how to channel your mental energy toward wealth creation, you accelerate your path to prosperity.

This chapter explores the power of focus and attention in attracting wealth. You'll learn how mental clarity plays a pivotal role in financial success, how to eliminate distractions that drain your energy and practical techniques for maintaining laser-sharp focus on your financial goals.

The Power of Focus and Its Role in Attracting Wealth

Focus is the mechanism by which we harness our mental resources. It's the process of directing attention and energy toward a single goal or task, allowing us to achieve extraordinary outcomes. In the context of wealth creation, focus is essential because it determines where your energy is invested. When you consistently focus on wealth-generating activities, you create momentum that pulls financial opportunities into your life.

One of the fundamental principles of focus is that whatever you give your attention to grows. This is known as the "law of attraction" in some circles, but it is grounded in real cognitive science. The brain's *reticular activating system* (RAS) filters the information you receive and brings to your attention what aligns with your current focus. If you are constantly focused on opportunities for growth and financial success, your RAS will filter out distractions and highlight opportunities that match your goals.

Conversely, if your attention is scattered—constantly thinking about obstacles, failures, or distractions—your brain will filter in information that reinforces those negative patterns. This is why many people feel stuck in a cycle of scarcity: their focus is directed toward problems rather than solutions.

In essence, your ability to attract wealth depends on what you choose to focus on. Focus is like sunlight through a magnifying glass: when diffused, the sunlight is warm but lacks power. When focused, it can start a fire. The same principle applies to your mental energy: scattered thoughts and inconsistent attention lead to mediocre results, while focusing on financial success creates powerful momentum.

Mental Clarity: The Foundation of Financial Success

Mental clarity is the ability to think clearly, prioritize effectively, and make decisions aligned with your long-term goals. It's the foundation of focus and is critical in wealth creation.

Without mental clarity, it is easy to become overwhelmed, distracted, or lost in trivial tasks that do not contribute to financial success.

In today's fast-paced world, many people suffer from "mental clutter"—a state where their mind is bombarded with endless thoughts, worries, and distractions. This clutter blocks creativity, reduces productivity, and complicates focusing on the most critical actions. When your mind is cluttered, you're more likely to procrastinate, make impulsive decisions, or lose sight of your financial goals.

Achieving mental clarity is crucial because it allows you to channel your mental energy toward the right activities. It allows you to distinguish between urgent and essential tasks, enabling you to prioritize wealth-generating activities over distractions.

How Mental Clarity Drives Financial Success

1. **Enhanced Decision-Making**: When your mind is clear, you can make decisions based on logic and long-term strategy rather than emotions or short-term impulses. This is essential in managing investments, controlling spending, and identifying opportunities for financial growth.
2. **Increased Productivity**: Mental clarity eliminates the "mental fog" that often causes procrastination. When your mind is clear, you can focus on tasks without being bogged down by irrelevant thoughts or worries, leading to greater productivity.
3. **Reduced Stress**: A cluttered mind is a stressed mind. By achieving mental clarity, you reduce the mental noise that contributes to anxiety, allowing you to approach financial challenges with a calm and strategic mindset.
4. **Focus on Long-Term Goals**: Mental clarity helps you focus on the bigger picture. Instead of getting caught up in daily distractions or minor setbacks, you stay focused on your long-term financial goals.

Achieving mental clarity requires intentional practice. Let's explore some practical techniques for clearing your mind and focusing on wealth creation.

Eliminating Distractions: Focusing on What Truly Matters

Our attention is under siege in a world filled with constant distractions—social media, emails, phone notifications. Research shows that the average person is distracted every 11 minutes, and refocusing takes about 25 minutes after interruption. When it comes to wealth creation, these distractions are the enemies of focus. Whenever your attention is diverted from a wealth-generating activity, you lose valuable mental energy that could have been invested in achieving your financial goals.

One of the most critical financial success skills is learning to eliminate distractions and focus on what truly matters. Distractions are not just external (like notifications or emails); they are often internal as well, such as doubts, fears, or limiting beliefs that pull your focus away from wealth creation.

Types of Distractions

1. **External Distractions**: These include phone calls, emails, social media notifications, and interruptions from people around you. While some distractions are unavoidable, many can be managed by setting boundaries and creating focused work environments.
2. **Internal Distractions**: These include negative thoughts, self-doubt, procrastination, and fear of failure. Internal distractions are more insidious because they often go unnoticed but can severely undermine your ability to focus on your financial goals.

Techniques to Eliminate Distractions

1. **Set Clear Boundaries**: Create specific times during the day when you will focus on wealth-generating activities without distractions. Let others know you are unavailable during these periods, and turn off

notifications on your devices. This eliminates external distractions and helps you develop a focused, productive mindset.

2. **The Pomodoro Technique**: This time-management method involves working for a set period (usually 25 minutes) followed by a short break (5 minutes). After four "pomodoros," take a more extended break (15–30 minutes). This technique helps you maintain focus while preventing burnout. It also allows you to handle distractions in a structured way—during breaks rather than during focus sessions.

3. **Mindfulness and Meditation**: One of the most effective ways to eliminate internal distractions is through mindfulness meditation. By practicing mindfulness, you train your brain to focus on the present moment, which reduces mental clutter and improves your ability to concentrate. Regular meditation has been shown to increase gray matter in areas of the brain associated with focus, self-control, and emotional regulation.

4. **Identify and Address Internal Distractions**: Often, internal distractions stem from limiting beliefs or fears that prevent you from focusing on your financial goals. For example, you might avoid working on your budget because you're afraid of facing financial difficulties. Address these internal distractions by using techniques like journaling, therapy, or cognitive behavioral strategies to challenge and reframe limiting beliefs.

5. **Time Blocking**: This technique involves scheduling specific blocks of time during the day dedicated to focused work on wealth-generating activities. During these blocks, eliminate all non-essential activities and focus solely on your financial goals, whether it's researching investments, building a side business, or managing your finances. Time blocking creates a

structure that helps you stay accountable and avoid distractions.

Focusing on Wealth-Generating Activities

Not all tasks are created equal. One of the most crucial focus aspects is learning to distinguish between functions that generate wealth and those that waste time. Many people spend their days in busy work—tasks that feel productive but do little to move them closer to financial success. It's essential to focus on activities that directly contribute to economic growth to achieve wealth.

Wealth-Generating vs. Non-Wealth-Generating Activities

1. **Wealth-Generating Activities**: These tasks directly impact your financial well-being. They include investing, starting or growing a business, saving, budgeting, learning new financial skills, or networking with influential people in your industry. These tasks have a high return on investment (ROI) and should be a priority in your daily schedule.

2. **Non-Wealth-Generating Activities**: While they may seem significant, these tasks do not directly contribute to your financial success. Examples include checking social media, responding to non-urgent emails, attending unnecessary meetings, or engaging in passive entertainment. These activities often provide short-term satisfaction but have little or no long-term benefit to your financial goals.

The 80/20 Rule (Pareto Principle)

The 80/20 rule is a powerful principle in wealth creation. It states that 80% of your results come from 20% of your efforts. When it comes to focus, this means that only a small fraction of the activities you engage in each day are responsible for most of your financial success. The key is identifying which activities fall into the 20% and directing your focus toward them.

To apply the 80/20 rule to your financial life, analyze your daily tasks. Identify which tasks drive the most significant economic gains and which are merely distractions or busy work. Once you've identified your wealth-generating activities, focus most of your energy on those tasks. This simple shift in focus can dramatically accelerate your financial progress.

Exercises for Maintaining Laser-Sharp Focus on Financial Goals

The following exercises will help you develop and maintain a strong focus on wealth creation. Each exercise is designed to sharpen your ability to direct mental energy toward your financial goals while minimizing distractions.

Exercise 1: The Daily Focus Ritual

Every morning, set aside 10–15 minutes to align your mind with your financial goals for the day. This ritual will help set a clear intention for where you will direct your mental energy, ensuring you remain focused throughout the day.

1. **Start with a Clear Goal**: Write down your most important financial goal. This could be a long-term goal, such as growing your investment portfolio, or a short-term goal, like saving a specific amount by the end of the month. By writing down your goal each morning, you reinforce it in your mind.
2. **Prioritize Wealth-Generating Activities**: Identify the top three tasks you can accomplish today that will move you closer to your financial goal. These should

be wealth-generating activities, not busy work. Commit to completing these tasks before focusing on anything else.

3. **Visualization**: Close your eyes and spend a few minutes visualizing yourself successfully completing these tasks. See yourself taking confident steps, making progress, and experiencing the benefits of financial success. This mental rehearsal activates the neural pathways related to focus and goal achievement.

4. **Gratitude**: End your focus ritual with gratitude. Take a moment to acknowledge the financial resources you already have and the available opportunities. Gratitude reinforces abundance and opens your mind to new opportunities for growth.

By consistently performing this daily focus ritual, you'll notice an improvement in your ability to concentrate on wealth-building activities throughout the day.

Exercise 2: The Distraction Detox

This exercise eliminates distractions from your daily routine, allowing you to focus more intently on your financial goals.

1. **Identify Your Biggest Distractions**: Spend one day tracking how you spend your time. Identify the most common distractions that prevent you from engaging in wealth-generating activities, such as social media, unnecessary emails, or internal distractions like negative thinking.

2. **Set Boundaries**: Create clear boundaries once you've identified your biggest distractions. External distractions might mean setting specific times when you check emails or social media and turning off notifications during focused work sessions. Use mindfulness techniques to observe negative thoughts without engaging with them for internal distractions.

3. **Create a Focus-Friendly Environment**: Adjust your environment to support focus. Remove physical clutter from your workspace and set up a dedicated space for financial tasks. A clutter-free, distraction-free environment helps your brain focus on the task at hand.

4. **Implement Focus Blocks**: Use time-blocking techniques to create uninterrupted periods of deep work on wealth-generating activities. During these focus blocks, eliminate all distractions and concentrate solely on your financial goals.

5. **Evaluate Progress**: After one week, evaluate how eliminating distractions has impacted your ability to focus. Are you accomplishing more wealth-generating activities? Have you noticed an increase in productivity? Continue refining your distraction detox process as needed.

Exercise 3: The 30-Day Wealth Focus Challenge

This 30-day challenge will help you build a long-term habit of focusing on wealth creation.

1. **Set a 30-Day Financial Goal**: Choose a specific financial goal you want to achieve in the next 30 days. It could be increasing your savings, paying off debt, launching a side hustle, or building your investment portfolio.

2. **Daily Wealth-Generating Activity**: Commit to spending at least one hour each day focused on activities that directly contribute to achieving your goal.

3. Whether researching investment opportunities, creating a budget, or building a business, the key is consistent action.

4. **Track Your Progress**: Document the activities you completed and your progress toward your daily goal.

This will help you stay accountable and provide insight into how your focused efforts are paying off.

5. **Reflect and Adjust**: At the end of each week, reflect on what's working and what's not. Are there specific distractions or obstacles that are hindering your progress? Adjust your strategy to maintain focus on the most productive activities.

6. **Celebrate Your Success**: Review your progress at the end of the 30 days. Celebrate your achievements and set a new financial goal to keep the momentum going. By building this habit of focus, you'll train your brain to seek out and seize opportunities for continuous wealth creation.

Maintaining Focus in the Long Term: The Path to Sustained Financial Success

The power of focus is not something that produces results overnight. However, with consistent practice, you will notice significant changes in how you approach wealth creation. Over time, your ability to direct mental energy toward wealth-generating activities will become second nature.

Maintaining long-term focus is not just about setting goals. It's about discipline, self-awareness, and a deep commitment to personal growth. These qualities are the foundation of your financial success. Here are a few strategies to help you stay focused on your financial goals over the long term:

1. **Review and Adjust Your Goals Regularly**: Reviewing and adjusting your goals is essential as you progress on your financial journey. What may have been a priority a year ago may no longer be relevant. Regularly assessing your financial goals ensures that your focus remains aligned with your evolving vision of success.
2. **Surround Yourself with Support**: Surrounding yourself with people who support your financial goals can significantly enhance your ability to focus. Whether it's a mentor, a financial advisor, or a mastermind group, having a support system keeps you accountable and motivated.
3. **Learn to Say No**: One of the most powerful tools for maintaining focus is the ability to say no. Learn to decline opportunities or activities not aligning with your financial goals. By saying no to distractions, you are saying yes to wealth creation.
4. **Invest in Continuous Learning**: Stay sharp by investing in your financial education. Attend workshops, read books, and learn from successful people in your field. The more you expand your knowledge, the better equipped you'll be to identify wealth-generating opportunities and remain focused on achieving your goals.

Final Thoughts: Focus as Your Most Powerful Wealth-Generating Tool

Focus is more than just the ability to concentrate on a task—it's the key to unlocking your full financial potential. By learning to direct your mental energy toward wealth-generating activities, you harness the full power of your mind to create opportunities, overcome challenges, and achieve financial success.

Remember, the journey toward wealth is not just about hard work—it's about working smart. It's about focusing on the activities that generate the most value and consistently aligning your thoughts, actions, and intentions with your financial goals.

Continue practicing the techniques you've learned in this chapter as you progress. Stay committed to eliminating distractions, maintaining mental clarity, and focusing on the wealth-generating activities that will drive you closer to your goals. With time, you'll develop the laser-sharp focus that separates the truly successful from the rest. The next chapter will explore practical financial strategies you can implement alongside your new focus skills, further accelerating your journey toward wealth and prosperity. You now have the mental tools—next, we'll look at how to apply them for maximum financial impact.

CHAPTER 6

Financial Visualization Manifesting Wealth Through Mental Imagery

Visualization is a powerful tool for wealth creation, rooted in the belief that if you can see it clearly in your mind, you can achieve it in reality. While often associated with athletes and high achievers, visualization is just as effective in personal finance. By consistently imagining your desired financial outcomes, you program your mind to seek opportunities that align with your vision and build the motivation to pursue them.

This chapter explores how visualization works, the scientific evidence supporting it, and how you can use visualization techniques to manifest wealth. By the end of this chapter, you'll have practical exercises that will help you harness the power of mental imagery to align your thoughts, actions, and behaviors with financial success.

The Power of Visualization for Wealth Creation

Visualization is the process of creating a mental image of a desired future outcome. It's more than just daydreaming—effective visualization involves vividly imagining specific goals, creating detailed mental pictures, and experiencing the emotions associated with achieving those goals. By regularly visualizing your financial success, you send powerful signals to your subconscious mind, reinforcing your commitment to achieving your goals. In monetary terms, visualization helps you clarify your economic desires. Many people struggle to reach their financial goals because they lack a clear picture of what those goals look like.

They may vaguely wish to "be wealthy" or "pay off debt," but without a vivid mental image, the brain lacks a specific target to focus on. Visualization gives your mind that target, enabling you to focus your energy on actions that align with your financial aspirations.

Visualization is not just a mental exercise. When you engage in visualization, you trigger a series of cognitive and neurological responses that impact your behavior. Research has shown that the brain cannot easily distinguish between real and imagined experiences. This means that when you vividly imagine yourself achieving financial success, your brain treats it as though it's already happening, which increases motivation and confidence.

The Science Behind Visualization and Goal Achievement

While visualization might sound like a new-age concept, there's solid scientific evidence behind its effectiveness. Neuroscientific research into how the brain processes imagery shows that visualization can profoundly impact behavior and performance. This is because when we visualize something, we activate the same neural circuits that are involved in actually performing that action.

Here are a few key findings from the science of visualization:

1. Neural Activation

When you visualize yourself achieving a financial goal—whether it's receiving a bonus, paying off debt, or making a successful investment—the brain activates the neural circuits involved in achieving that goal. This activation strengthens the connection between intention and action, making it more likely that you will take steps toward realizing your financial vision.

Studies have shown that the brain's *prefrontal cortex*, which is responsible for decision-making and planning, becomes highly active during visualization. This brain region helps translate goals into actionable steps, ensuring that day-to-day actions align with long-term vision.

2. The Placebo Effect

The placebo effect demonstrates how powerful belief can be in shaping reality. In medical studies, patients given a sugar pill but told it's a potent medication often experience real improvements in their health. This phenomenon occurs because the mind accepts the belief as reality, prompting the body to act accordingly. Visualization operates similarly: by mentally rehearsing financial success, you trick your brain into believing that success is inevitable, making it easier to take actions aligned with that belief.

3. The Reticular Activating System (RAS)

The brain's *reticular activating system* (RAS) is a network of neurons responsible for filtering information and focusing on what's important. The RAS plays a significant role in visualization because it helps you zero in on opportunities that match your mental picture of success. Once you've visualized a specific financial goal, your RAS will start to notice opportunities, resources, and ideas that can help you achieve it, many of which you might have overlooked.

For example, suppose you visualize building a successful business. In that case, your RAS will filter through the overwhelming information around you to focus on relevant ideas, conversations, and connections to your goal. Visualization programs your brain to focus on what matters most, making the path to financial success clearer and more accessible.

Visualization Exercises for Financial Success

Practicing visualization regularly is important to make it a practical tool for wealth creation. The following exercises will guide you through creating vivid mental images of your desired financial future and help you align your daily actions with those images.

Exercise 1: Creating Your Financial Vision Board

A financial vision board is a physical or digital collection of images and words representing your financial goals. This exercise externalizes your visualization practice, making your mental images more concrete.

1. **Gather Materials**: To make a physical vision board, gather magazines, scissors, glue, and a poster board. If you prefer a digital version, use a platform like Pinterest or Canva.
2. **Select Images that Represent Financial Goals**: Find images, quotes, and words that resonate with your financial goals. These could include pictures of your dream home, symbols of wealth, vacations you want to take, or financial milestones like paying off a loan.
3. **Visualize Each Image**: As you place each image on your vision board, close your eyes and visualize yourself achieving that goal. What does it feel like to reach that milestone? Who is with you? What emotions are you experiencing? The more vividly you can imagine these moments, the more powerful the exercise becomes.
4. **Place Your Vision Board Somewhere Visible**: Keep your vision board where you'll see it every day—whether in your office, on your phone, or as a desktop wallpaper. Each time you look at it, take a moment to rehearse achieving your goals mentally.

This exercise reinforces your financial desires and reminds you of your work. By consistently focusing on your vision board, you keep your financial goals in mind and align your actions accordingly.

Exercise 2: The Future Self Visualization

This exercise will help you visualize yourself as the successful, wealthy person you aspire to become. By mentally rehearsing your future success, you train your brain to adopt the habits and behaviors that will lead to financial prosperity.

1. **Find a Quiet Space**: Sit comfortably, close your eyes, and take a few deep breaths. Relax your body and quiet your mind.
2. **Visualize Your Future Self**: Imagine yourself 5 or 10 years in the future. You've achieved your financial goals, and you're living the life of your dreams. What does your day look like? Where do you live? What kind of work do you do? How do you feel knowing that you've created wealth and financial security?
3. **Engage All Your Senses**: The more vividly you can picture this version of yourself, the more powerful the visualization will be. Engage all your senses—what do you see, hear, smell, and feel in this future scenario? Are you living in your dream home, traveling the world, or enjoying financial freedom?
4. **Step Into Your Future Self**: Now imagine stepping into this version of yourself. Feel the confidence, security, and abundance that comes from achieving your financial goals. As you embody your future self, notice how your posture, emotions, and mindset change.
5. **Ask for Guidance**: In your visualization, ask your future self for advice on how to achieve financial success. What habits, decisions, or actions helped them reach this

point? What can you start doing today to get closer to your future self's level of success?

6. **End with Gratitude**: Conclude the visualization by thanking your future self for their guidance. Open your eyes and carry the energy of your future self with you as you move through your day.

Regularly practicing this future self-visualization aligns your current actions with the successful person you aspire to become. By mentally rehearsing your success, you program your mind to act in ways that support your financial goals.

Exercise 3: Visualization for Daily Financial Focus

This exercise is designed to help you focus on your financial goals daily by visualizing success at the start of each day.

1. **Morning Visualization**: Before you begin your workday, spend 5 minutes visualizing one specific financial goal you want to accomplish each morning. It could be anything from increasing your savings to closing a new business deal.

2. **Vividly Picture the Outcome**: Imagine the moment you successfully achieve the goal. How will you feel when you reach that milestone? Picture the exact steps you'll take throughout the day to get closer to achieving it.

3. **Visualize Overcoming Obstacles**: Anticipate any challenges or distractions that might come up during the day. In your visualization, see yourself confidently overcoming these obstacles and staying on track with your financial goal.

4. **Embrace the Feeling of Success**: As you visualize your day unfolding, focus on accomplishment and financial security. The emotions you attach to your

visualization will help reinforce the behavior you need to succeed.

Starting each day with a clear mental picture of your financial goals sets the tone for focused, intentional action.

Keeping a Vivid Picture of Your Desired Financial Future in Mind

The key to successful visualization is repetition and emotional engagement. The more frequently you visualize your financial goals—and the more vividly you imagine the emotions of achieving them—the stronger the impact on your subconscious mind. Visualization works best when it becomes a daily habit, keeping your goals at the forefront of your mind and aligning your thoughts and actions with your desired financial future.

Here are a few tips for keeping a vivid picture of your financial future in mind:

1. **Schedule Regular Visualization Sessions**: Set aside time each day for visualization. Whether it's during your morning routine or before bed, making

Keeping a Vivid Picture of Your Desired Financial Future in Mind (Continued)

1. **Schedule Regular Visualization Sessions**: Set aside time each day for visualization. Whether during your morning routine or before bed, making visualization a consistent part of your schedule will help you focus on your financial goals. The more you visualize, the clearer and more detailed your mental image will become, reinforcing your commitment to wealth creation.
2. **Incorporate Visualization into Daily Activities**: Visualization should not be a separate, formal practice.

You can incorporate it into your daily activities. For example, while commuting, mentally rehearse your financial success. While exercising or cooking, take a few minutes to picture yourself achieving your financial goals. By making visualization a natural part of your day, you ensure that your mind remains focused on wealth creation even during routine tasks.

3. **Use Visualization as a Motivational Tool**: Return to your visualization practice whenever you feel discouraged or encounter setbacks. Imagine yourself overcoming the challenges and still reaching your financial goals. This can be a powerful way to stay motivated and maintain perspective during tough times. Visualization reminds you that temporary obstacles are just stepping stones to financial success.

4. **Keep a Visual Reminder of Your Goals**: Whether it's your vision board, a digital background, or a list of your financial goals, having a physical reminder in your environment can strengthen your visualization practice. Each time you see the reminder, take a moment to mentally rehearse the achievement of those goals. This keeps your desired financial future at the top of your mind throughout the day.

The Role of Emotion in Effective Visualization

Visualization is most powerful when paired with strong, positive emotions. Emotions are the glue that makes your mental imagery stick in your subconscious mind. When you visualize achieving your financial goals, it's not enough to see the images—you must also feel the emotions associated with those achievements.

Neuroscience shows that emotions significantly enhance the brain's ability to form and strengthen neural pathways. When you visualize financial success, attach strong feelings of excitement, gratitude, pride, and confidence to your mental images. By engaging these emotions, you condition your mind to seek out situations and opportunities that align with those feelings.

The more vividly you feel these emotions during your visualization sessions, the more your brain becomes wired for success. Over time, your brain will naturally gravitate toward actions that match the emotional energy of wealth and abundance.

Final Thoughts: Visualization as a Lifelong Wealth-Building Tool

Financial visualization is not a one-time exercise; it's a lifelong tool for aligning your mind with the wealth you want to create. The more consistently you practice visualization, the more naturally you will see opportunities for financial growth and success. Visualization shifts your mindset from scarcity to abundance and helps you focus on your goals despite obstacles.

Remember, visualization is not a substitute for action but a catalyst for it. By keeping a vivid picture of your desired financial future in mind, you motivate yourself to take the necessary steps to turn that vision into reality. Whether you're looking to grow your savings, build a business, or reach financial independence, visualization helps you create a mental blueprint for success.

In the next chapter, we'll explore practical financial strategies that complement your visualization practice. You've learned how to condition your mind for success, and now we'll explore how to apply that mindset to real-world financial decisions and actions.

CHAPTER 7

Cultivating Abundance Shifting from Scarcity to Limitless Thinking

The concept of abundance extends far beyond material wealth. It's a mindset, a way of viewing the world that transcends financial gain and encompasses how we approach opportunities, relationships, and personal growth. In contrast, the scarcity mindset views life through a lens of limitation and lack. This chapter is designed to help you recognize when scarcity-driven thinking is holding you back and guide you toward embracing an abundance mindset. By cultivating this shift, you'll open the doors to greater financial success and create a more fulfilling and opportunity-rich life.

This chapter will explore the distinction between scarcity and abundance mindsets, show you how to recognize scarcity-driven thoughts, and provide actionable strategies for shifting toward limitless thinking. By the end of this chapter, you'll have practical tools to cultivate a mindset that allows you to thrive in every area of life.

The Difference Between a Scarcity Mindset and an Abundance Mindset

A **scarce mindset** is rooted in the belief that resources—money, opportunities, success, or even happiness—are limited. People with a scarcity mindset often fear that there isn't enough to go around, leading them to compete for limited resources, hold onto what they have, and avoid risks. This way of thinking can severely limit financial and personal growth because it focuses on fear and lack.

Conversely, an **abundance mindset** operates from the belief that there is plenty for everyone. People with an abundance mindset trust that opportunities, resources, and success are limitless, allowing them to approach challenges with confidence and an open mind. They believe that success is not a zero-sum game, and just because one person achieves wealth or success, it doesn't mean there is less available for others. This perspective fosters collaboration, creativity, and a proactive approach to financial growth.

Understanding the distinction between these two mindsets is essential because how you think about the world influences your actions. With a scarcity mindset, you might avoid taking financial risks or sabotaging opportunities because you fear losing what little you have. With an abundance mindset, you are more likely to embrace opportunities, invest in yourself, and take calculated risks that lead to greater rewards.

Key Characteristics of a Scarcity Mindset

1. **Fear of Losing What You Have**: People with a scarcity mindset often fear that any financial, personal, or professional risk might lead to loss. As a result, they avoid stepping outside their comfort zone, which prevents them from experiencing economic growth.
2. **Short-Term Thinking**: A scarcity mindset focuses on immediate needs and short-term gains, often at the expense of long-term planning.
3. For example, someone with a scarcity mindset might prioritize quick financial fixes over investments with long-term wealth-building potential.
4. **Jealousy and Comparison**: Scarcity thinking fosters a belief that there isn't enough success, leading to jealousy and comparison. People with a scarcity mindset may feel threatened by others' success, assuming it diminishes their chances of achieving wealth.

5. **Self-Limiting Beliefs**: Scarcity thinking reinforces limiting beliefs, such as "I'm not good enough," "I'll never have enough," or "Success is for other people, not me." These beliefs trap individuals in a cycle of self-doubt and inaction.

Key Characteristics of an Abundance Mindset

1. **Belief in Infinite Possibilities**: People with an abundance mindset believe there is always more—more opportunities, more success, more money—available to them. This belief empowers them to take risks and pursue ambitious goals.
2. **Long-Term Thinking**: An abundance mindset is future-focused, prioritizing long-term growth and financial security over short-term gains. People with this mindset will invest time, energy, and resources into building sustainable wealth.
3. **Gratitude**: Many thinkers focus on what they have rather than what they lack. They practice gratitude for their current resources and opportunities, reinforcing a sense of abundance and attracting wealth into their lives.
4. **Collaborative and Generous**: People with an abundance mindset understand collaboration leads to greater success. They're generous with their knowledge, time, and resources, knowing that giving to others doesn't diminish their potential for success.

How to Recognize Scarcity-Driven Thoughts

Scarcity thinking is often profoundly ingrained and can be difficult to recognize initially. However, once you become aware of the signs, you can challenge and shift these thoughts to an abundance-driven perspective. Here are some common indicators that your thoughts are rooted in scarcity:

1. Fear-Based Decision Making

When making decisions out of fear—especially fear of loss or failure—you're likely operating from a scarcity mindset. For example, if you avoid investing because you're afraid of losing money, you're focusing on the potential for loss rather than the growth potential.

2. Constant Worry About Money

If you constantly worry about money, even when you're financially stable, this is a sign of scarcity thinking. People with a scarcity mindset often feel like there's never enough, no matter how much they have.

3. Hesitation to Share or Collaborate

People with a scarcity mindset often hesitate to share knowledge, opportunities, or resources with others because they fear doing so will leave them with less. They see success as a limited resource rather than something that can grow through collaboration.

4. Avoidance of Risks

A significant indicator of scarcity thinking is the avoidance of risks. If you find yourself shying away from new opportunities—applying for a higher-paying job, starting a business, or investing in yourself—it could be because you're operating from a belief that you have too much to lose and not enough to gain.

Shifting from Scarcity to an Abundance Mindset

Recognizing scarcity-driven thoughts is the first step but shifting them to an abundance mindset requires conscious effort and practice. Here are key strategies to help you transition from a mindset of lack to one of abundance:

1. Reframe Negative Thoughts

When you think from a place of scarcity, reframe the thought into a positive, abundance-focused perspective. For example, if you think, "I can't afford that," try shifting it to, "How can I afford that?" This simple shift opens your mind to possibilities rather than focusing on limitations.

Reframing scarcity-driven thoughts allows you to train your brain to see solutions instead of problems. Over time, this rewires your thought patterns to align with an abundance-driven perspective.

2. Practice Gratitude Daily

Gratitude is one of the most effective ways to cultivate an abundance mindset. By focusing on what you already have, you shift your attention away from lack and toward abundance. Regularly practicing gratitude helps train your brain to recognize the wealth of opportunities, resources, and successes already in your life.

Each day, write down three things you're grateful for, especially in your financial life. It could be as simple as paying your bills, having access to education, or experiencing support from friends and family. The more you focus on gratitude, the more you'll see life through a lens of abundance.

3. Set Long-Term Financial Goals

Scarcity thinking often leads to short-term financial decisions, such as focusing on immediate expenses without planning for future growth. To shift to an abundance mindset, begin setting long-term financial goals that reflect your vision for wealth and prosperity.

Whether saving for retirement, building a portfolio, or buying real estate, setting long-term goals helps you focus on the bigger picture. This approach encourages you to think beyond immediate needs and fosters an abundant view of your financial future.

4. Take Calculated Risks

A scarcity mindset keeps you locked in place, afraid to take risks for fear of losing what you have. An abundance mindset encourages you to take calculated risks, understanding that you'll learn from the experience and grow even if you face setbacks.

Start by taking small risks, whether it's investing a little more in the stock market, launching a side hustle, or pursuing a higher-paying job. Each time you take a risk, your brain becomes more accustomed to operating from abundance, reinforcing the belief that there is always more to gain.

Abundance as a Holistic Mindset

It's important to remember that abundance is not just about money. While financial success is a key part of an abundance mindset, it's also about how you view life, relationships, and opportunities. When you cultivate a mindset of abundance, you recognize that wealth comes in many forms, including knowledge, time, relationships, and personal growth.

1. Abundance in Opportunities

People with an abundance mindset see the world as full of opportunities. They don't fear missing out because they believe that new chances for success are constantly emerging. This perspective allows them to act without hesitation, knowing there will always be another, even if one opportunity doesn't work out.

2. Abundance in Relationships

Abundance thinking also extends to relationships. People with this mindset understand that strong, supportive relationships are a form of wealth. They nurture connections, collaborate, and support others, knowing that success multiplies when shared. Helping others achieve their goals creates an environment of mutual growth and abundance.

3. Abundance in Growth

An abundance mindset is growth oriented. People with this mindset are committed to lifelong learning and personal development. They seek out knowledge, challenge themselves, and embrace change, knowing that growth is essential to creating a fulfilling and prosperous life.

Exercises to Cultivate an Abundance Mindset

Shifting to an abundance mindset takes practice, but these exercises will help you rewire your brain to see the world as full of possibilities and wealth:

Exercise 1: The Abundance Journal

Daily journaling is a powerful way to train your mind to focus on abundance. Writing down positive experiences and thoughts daily reinforces the belief that life is full of opportunities and wealth.

1. **Create an Abundance Journal**: Dedicate a journal to documenting moments of abundance in your life. These could be financial gains, personal achievements, or moments of feeling fortunate or grateful.
2. **Write Daily Entries**: At the end of each day, write down three things that made you feel abundant. They can be small, such as a productive meeting, or significant, like paying off a debt. The goal is to train your mind to focus on what's going well and growing in your life.
3. **Reflect on Your Progress**: After one month, look back through your journal. Notice how your perspective has shifted. By focusing on abundance, you'll notice more opportunities in your daily life, reinforcing the cycle of positive, growth-oriented thinking.

Exercise 2: Reframe Your Limiting Beliefs

Limiting beliefs are thoughts that create a mental barrier to success. These beliefs are often rooted in scarcity and prevent us from seeing the world as full of possibilities. This exercise will help you identify and reframe those beliefs to align with abundance.

1. **Identify Your Limiting Beliefs**: Write down common limiting thoughts you have about money, success, or opportunities. Examples might include: "There's never enough money," "I'm not good at managing finances," or "Opportunities like that don't happen to people like me."
2. **Challenge and Reframe**: Next to each limiting belief, write a new statement reflecting an abundance mindset. For example, reframe "There's never enough money" to "There are limitless ways for me to earn and grow wealth." Reframing these beliefs helps create new neural pathways focusing on possibility rather than limitation.
3. **Practice Daily**: When you think of a scarcity-driven thought, pause and reframe it. This practice, done consistently, rewires your brain to default to abundant thinking over time.

Exercise 3: Collaborate for Growth

Scarcity thinking often leads to isolation, while abundance thinking fosters collaboration. This exercise will help you develop a habit of collaborating with others to amplify growth opportunities.

1. **Identify an Area for Collaboration**: Think of a project, goal, or financial venture where you can involve someone else. This could be a business idea, investment

opportunity, or personal growth goal where working with another person can bring mutual benefits.

2. **Reach Out**: Reach out to a colleague, mentor, or friend to explore ways to collaborate. This could involve sharing knowledge and resources or supporting each other's progress. Approach the conversation with the mindset that there is enough success to go around.

3. **Reflect on the Power of Collaboration**: Reflect on how the process expanded your view of what's possible after engaging in a collaborative effort. Collaboration, rooted in abundance, increases your chances of success and helps you see the endless possibilities of working together.

Exercise 4: Abundance Meditation

This meditation will help you grow in an abundant mindset and align your thoughts with limitless possibilities.

1. **Find a Quiet Space**: Sit comfortably and close your eyes. Take a few deep breaths to relax and center yourself.

2. **Visualize Abundance**: Imagine yourself surrounded by limitless opportunities. See doors opening around you, each leading to a new path of financial growth, personal success, or fulfilling relationships: picture money, opportunities, and wealth flowing toward you easily and effortlessly.

3. **Embrace the Feeling of Abundance**: Focus on the emotions that come with abundance. Feel the sense of security, confidence, and joy from knowing there is always more available to you. As you breathe, imagine yourself drawing in this feeling of abundance with each inhale.

4. **Carry the Feeling with You**: Remember that abundance is always available as you finish your

meditation. Throughout the day, bring this feeling of limitless possibility into every action and decision you make.

The Impact of an Abundance Mindset on Financial Success

The shift from a scarcity mindset to an abundance mindset can transform your financial life and overall well-being. When you train your mind to see the world as full of opportunities, you naturally align your behaviors with growth and success. This shift affects everything from how you approach investments to how you interact with others and handle setbacks.

Financial success becomes easier when you operate from a mindset of abundance because:

1. **Become Open to New Opportunities**: When you believe there is always more available, you are more likely to take advantage of the financial opportunities that come your way. Whether it's investing in a new business venture, negotiating a higher salary, or exploring passive income streams, you approach opportunities with confidence rather than fear.
2. **You Attract Success**: An abundance mindset shifts your energy. Rather than focusing on your lack, you exude a positive energy that attracts success.
3. People are drawn to work with those who radiate confidence and optimism, which creates more opportunities for collaboration and growth.
4. **Embrace Risk with Confidence**: Abundance thinkers are not afraid to take calculated risks because they trust that even if they experience setbacks, there are always more opportunities ahead. This allows them to make bolder financial decisions that often lead to greater rewards.

5. **You Focus on Growth**: With an abundance mindset, you focus on personal and financial growth rather than on holding onto what you have. This growth-oriented perspective encourages you to invest in yourself, learn new skills, and take steps that propel you toward greater wealth and success.

Creating a Life of Limitless Possibility

Shifting from scarcity to abundance is one of the most transformative changes you can make. This mindset shift empowers you to see the world not as a place of competition and lack but as a realm of endless opportunities and possibilities. Adopting an abundance mindset allows you to think bigger, take more intelligent risks, and confidently pursue financial success.

Remember, abundance is not just about money. It's a holistic way of viewing life—one where you trust that there is always more available, whether knowledge, opportunities, or wealth. As you continue to cultivate this mindset, you'll find that financial success becomes just one of many areas where you begin to experience more significant growth and fulfillment.

The next chapter will explore how to take your internal shifts—shifting to abundance thinking, visualization, and subconscious reprogramming—and apply them to real-world financial strategies that amplify your journey toward lasting wealth.

CHAPTER 8

The Power of Tithing, Giving to Receive Abundance

Tithing, a concept embedded in many spiritual and religious traditions, goes beyond simply giving away a portion of one's income. It is a powerful act that reflects one's trust in abundance, gratitude for what one has, and faith that more will come. Tithing is much more than financial transactions; it involves one's heart, mind, and spirit.

Initially, the idea of tithing may seem contradictory. In a culture that often encourages saving, accumulating, and holding onto what we have out of fear of scarcity, giving away 10% of your income can create uncertainty. But when approached from a mindset of abundance, tithing is not about what you lose—it's about what you gain: freedom, peace, and the opportunity to participate in the flow of wealth.

The Cycle of Giving and Receiving

When we give regularly, we reinforce the principle that wealth flows. By giving, we open channels for spiritual and material prosperity to flow in and out of our lives. Tithing reminds us that we are not the ultimate owners of our possessions; we are stewards entrusted with resources to use responsibly for our and others' benefit.

Successful individuals, from business owners to spiritual leaders, recognize the importance of this practice. For them, giving is a key that unlocks more opportunities. When we release what we have with generosity, we allow something greater to return to us. Instead of holding onto money out of fear of losing it, tithing teaches that releasing it with an open-heart plants seeds that will bear fruit in unexpected ways.

Transforming Fear into Trust

One of the biggest obstacles to tithing is fear of not having enough and fear that our needs won't be met if we give. But by giving, even when it seems difficult, we cultivate deep trust in the universe's abundance. It is an act of faith that declares: "I trust that I will always have enough. There is no scarcity, only abundance."

Practicing tithing from a place of trust transforms your relationship with money. It shifts your mindset from fear to faith, from lack to abundance. You begin to trust that by participating in the cycle of giving, you are part of something much more significant and align yourself with the natural flow of prosperity.

Tithing as a Practice of Gratitude

Tithing is also a powerful practice of gratitude. It forces you to pause and reflect on all that you have. Financial stress often blinds us to our blessings. By giving away a portion of your earnings, you consciously acknowledge that you have been blessed, regardless of your circumstances.

More recognition shifts your perspective, transforming what might feel like "not enough" into "more than enough."

In giving, you help others and reprogram your mind to focus on abundance instead of lack. This mindset of gratitude raises your emotional vibration, attracting more abundance into your life.

How to Start Tithing

If you've never practiced tithing, starting can feel daunting. But like any new practice, the key is to begin with intention and heart.

1. **Choose a Percentage That Feels Right**: While traditional tithing suggests 10%, the most important thing is to give an amount that feels good to you. If 10% feels too much, start smaller and increase as you grow more comfortable.
2. **Give to Causes That Inspire You**: Tithing is most powerful when you feel emotionally connected to what you are supporting. Choose organizations or causes that resonate with your values and have a positive impact.
3. **Be Consistent**: The impact of tithing comes from regular, consistent giving. Whether weekly, monthly, or annually, stay committed to your practice and observe how your mindset shifts.

The real power of tithing lies in consistency. It's not about a one-time large donation, but the ongoing, regular act of giving that shifts your mindset and relationship with abundance. Consistency is key whether you give weekly, monthly, or annually. Over time, you'll notice how your mentality towards money and abundance evolves.

Let Go of Control

A critical aspect of tithing is releasing the expectation of what you will receive in return. Tithing is not a transactional act—it's an expression of faith and gratitude. Trust that the blessings will return to you unexpectedly, often far beyond financial measures. Giving is a celebration of abundance, not a contract with the universe to expect immediate rewards. When you let go of control and release your gifts freely, you align with the flow of abundance and allow it to return in its way and timing.

The Spiritual Wealth of Tithing

Tithing is not just about material wealth—it's also about spiritual growth. Giving connects you to something larger than yourself, fostering a sense of community, compassion, and shared purpose. You become a part of the greater good, using your resources to uplift and support others. Through this practice, you're enhancing your financial well-being and contributing to society's well-being.

Money is just a tool—a resource that can flow and circulate when we trust that there is enough for everyone. When you give, you help others thrive and open the space for prosperity to return to you in unexpected and blessed ways.

Conclusion: Giving to Receive

Tithing is a practice that profoundly transforms one's relationship with money, abundance, and spiritual connection. By incorporating this practice into one's life, one not only contributes to the well-being of others but also strengthens one's belief in the universe's infinite abundance.

Remember, the more you give, the more you receive—not because you demand it, but because opening your heart and your resources aligns you with life's natural flow, where there is always enough for everyone.

Through this act of generosity, you will begin to experience the true power of money as a tool for good, not just in your life but also in the lives of those around you.

CHAPTER 8

Emotional Mastery Aligning Feelings with Financial Goals

Money is more than numbers in a bank account or material possessions—it is intricately connected to our emotions. Our feelings about money often determine how we manage it, attract it, and ultimately, how successful we become in building wealth. Fear, doubt, and anxiety can keep us stuck in a cycle of financial scarcity, while emotions like confidence, gratitude, and joy can help us align with financial abundance. This chapter will explore the powerful connection between emotions and money and how mastering your emotions can lead to economic success.

We'll delve into emotional regulation techniques that help maintain a high-frequency emotional state, explain how negative emotions can block financial growth, and offer strategies to develop emotional intelligence around money. By the end of this chapter, you'll have practical tools to align your emotional state with your financial goals.

The Connection Between Emotions and Money

Emotions are deeply tied to how we perceive and interact with money. For many people, emotions like fear, guilt, and shame shape their financial decisions, leading to avoiding financial planning, overspending, or not taking necessary risks for growth. On the other hand, positive emotions like confidence, joy, and gratitude can help attract financial opportunities, encourage intelligent decision-making, and create a mindset open to wealth.

The reason for this connection lies in how our brain processes emotions. The *limbic system*, often called the brain's emotional center, is where our emotions arise. This part of the brain has a direct influence on decision-making, especially when it comes to finances. When emotions are not well-regulated, they can cloud judgment, leading to impulsive decisions or a failure to take necessary risks. Conversely, when we are emotionally balanced, we are more likely to make decisions that align with our financial goals.

Let's explore two examples of how emotions can influence financial behavior:

>1. **Fear and Avoidance**: Fear of losing money can lead to avoidance behaviors, such as not investing in opportunities that could lead to long-term growth or avoiding financial planning altogether. This is a survival response from the brain, which perceives any financial risk as a potential threat. The problem is that avoiding financial decisions out of fear prevents progress and keeps people stuck in their current economic situation.
>
>2. **Confidence and Risk-Taking**: On the flip side, confidence allows individuals to take calculated risks that lead to financial growth. When you feel confident in managing money and making wise decisions, you are more likely to invest in opportunities, ask for a raise, or pursue a new business venture. Confidence aligns your actions with the belief that financial success is achievable.

Emotional mastery is key to aligning your feelings with your financial goals. By understanding and regulating your emotions, you can make decisions that support your financial success rather than hinder it.

Emotional Regulation: The Key to Attracting Wealth

To attract wealth, it's essential to maintain a high-frequency emotional state. Emotions such as joy, gratitude, and confidence are often associated with abundance and prosperity. These emotions resonate at higher frequencies and help you align with financial success. When you're in a positive emotional state, you're more likely to notice opportunities, take smart risks, and make decisions that lead to wealth.

On the other hand, low-frequency emotions like fear, doubt, and anxiety block financial growth. These emotions cause you to focus on scarcity and loss, preventing you from seeing the abundance of opportunities around you.

The goal is not to eliminate negative emotions entirely—everyone experiences fear or anxiety at times—but to regulate these emotions so they don't control your financial decisions. Emotional regulation techniques help you stay in a positive, abundant mindset even when challenges arise.

Techniques for Emotional Regulation

Emotional regulation is managing your emotions, especially in stressful or challenging situations. Here are some proven techniques to help you maintain a high-frequency emotional state and align with wealth:

1. Mindfulness and Meditation

Mindfulness is the practice of being present in the moment without judgment. When you practice mindfulness, you become more aware of your emotional state and can respond to financial challenges calmly rather than impulsively.

How to Practice Mindfulness:

- Set aside a few minutes daily to sit quietly and focus on your breath. Notice any thoughts or emotions that arise without getting attached to them.
- As you practice, become aware of how specific financial thoughts or worries make you feel. Acknowledge these emotions without letting them control you.
- Mindfulness helps you pause before reacting to a financial decision, allowing you to approach it with a balanced emotional state.

Meditation, especially gratitude meditation, can also shift your emotional frequency. By focusing on gratitude, you train your brain to recognize the abundance already in your life, creating an emotional foundation of joy and contentment.

2. Reframing Negative Emotions

Negative emotions, such as fear or anxiety about money, often stem from limiting beliefs or past experiences. Reframing these emotions involves changing the way you interpret and respond to them.

For example, if you feel anxious about investing because you fear losing money, reframe the situation by focusing on the potential for growth and learning. Instead of seeing the investment as a risk, view it as an opportunity to expand your financial knowledge and potentially increase your wealth.

Steps to Reframe Negative Emotions:

- Identify your specific emotion (e.g., fear, anxiety, doubt).

- Ask yourself: What belief or thought is causing this emotion? Is it realistic or based on fear?
- Reframe the belief in a way that supports growth. For example, "I might lose money" can become "Every investment is a learning experience that brings me closer to financial success."

Reframing negative emotions shifts your focus from scarcity and loss to growth and opportunity.

3. Emotional Anchoring

Emotional anchoring is a technique for using a physical or mental "anchor" to bring yourself back to a positive emotional state. It is especially useful when dealing with financial stress or fear.

How to Use Emotional Anchoring:

- Think of a moment when you felt incredibly confident and successful. This could be a time when you achieved a personal or financial goal.
- Create a physical anchor—such as touching your thumb and forefinger together—while focusing on the emotions of that moment. This anchors the positive emotion to the physical gesture.
- When you feel anxious or stressed about money, use your anchor to bring back those positive feelings of confidence and success. This helps you make financial decisions from a place of strength rather than fear.

4. Gratitude Practice

Gratitude is one of the most powerful emotions for attracting wealth. When you focus on what you already have, you shift your energy away from scarcity and toward abundance. Gratitude opens your mind to see more growth opportunities, and it helps you feel more secure in your current financial situation.

How to Practice Gratitude for Financial Success:

- Keep a gratitude journal where you write down at least three things you're grateful for each day, specifically related to money or financial opportunities. This could be as simple as being grateful for a steady paycheck, the ability to pay bills or unexpected financial blessings.
- Each time you feel stressed or anxious about money, pause and reflect on what's going well financially. This practice shifts your focus to abundance, creating a positive emotional foundation for wealth.

How Fear, Doubt, and Anxiety Block Financial Success

Negative emotions like fear, doubt, and anxiety create mental and emotional barriers to wealth. When caught in a cycle of fear, it isn't easy to act, recognize opportunities, or make sound financial decisions. These emotions trigger the brain's *amygdala*, responsible for the fight-or-flight response. In this state, your body is primed for survival, not for taking calculated risks or making strategic financial moves.

Here's how each emotion can block financial success:

1. Fear

Fear is one of the biggest obstacles to wealth creation. Fear of losing money, failure, and making the wrong decision can cause paralysis and prevent you from acting. Fear often leads to missed opportunities, as people hesitate to invest, negotiate, or pursue new ventures.

How to Overcome Fear:

- Reframe fear as a sign of growth. Whenever you feel afraid to take a financial step, remind yourself that fear often arises when you're stepping out of your comfort zone, which is where growth happens.
- Break down financial decisions into smaller, manageable steps. This reduces the overwhelming nature of big decisions and allows you to act, even in the face of fear.

2. Doubt

Doubt undermines your confidence in managing money or achieving financial success. It often comes from past failures or negative experiences with money. You're less likely to take bold steps toward your financial goals when you doubt yourself.

How to Overcome Doubt:

- Challenge your self-doubt by reflecting on past successes. Remind yourself of times when you made smart financial decisions or overcame challenges.
- Surround yourself with positive influences, such as financial mentors or supportive peers, who reinforce your belief in your financial abilities.

3. Anxiety

Anxiety about money often stems from uncertainty and the feeling that one doesn't have control over one's financial situation. This can lead to avoidance behaviors, like not checking one's bank account or avoiding financial planning altogether.

How to Overcome Anxiety:

- Take small, proactive steps toward gaining control over your finances. For example, schedule weekly to review your budget, pay bills, or track expenses. By acting, you reduce the feeling of uncertainty that fuels anxiety.
- Practice deep breathing or mindfulness techniques when anxiety about money arises. This helps calm the nervous system, allowing you to approach your finances with clarity and focus.

Practical Strategies to Develop Emotional Intelligence Regarding Money

Emotional intelligence (EQ) is the ability to recognize, understand, and manage one's emotions and those of others. In the context of financial success, developing emotional intelligence helps one make better money-related decisions, manage stress, and build resilience in the face of financial challenges.

Here are several practical strategies to develop emotional intelligence around money:

1. Build Self-Awareness

The first step in emotional mastery is understanding your emotional patterns around money. Self-awareness allows you to recognize when negative emotions like fear, doubt, or guilt arise, giving you the power to manage them rather than being controlled by them.

How to Build Self-Awareness:

- Pay attention to how you feel during financial activities, such as paying bills, discussing money, or making investments. What emotions arise? Are they positive or negative?
- Journal about your financial decisions and reflect on how your emotions influenced them. This practice helps you identify emotional patterns that may be holding you back.

2. Cultivate Self-Regulation

Self-regulation is managing one's emotions, especially in stressful or challenging situations. For example, if one receives an unexpected bill, self-regulation allows one to stay calm, assess the situation, and create a plan rather than panicking.

How to Cultivate Self-Regulation:

- Practice the emotional regulation techniques mentioned earlier, such as mindfulness, emotional reframing, and gratitude. These techniques help you stay grounded during financial ups and downs.
- Before making a significant financial decision, take a moment to pause, breathe, and check in with your emotional state. Are you acting out of fear or confidence? Self-regulation lets you choose the emotional response that best aligns with your financial goals.

3. Develop Empathy in Financial Relationships

Emotional intelligence isn't just about managing your emotions; it also involves understanding and responding to the emotions of others. This is especially important in financial relationships, whether it's with a spouse, business partner, or financial advisor.

How to Develop Empathy:

- When discussing money with others, practice active listening. Acknowledge their emotions and concerns without judgment. This helps build trust and fosters better financial collaboration.
- Approach financial conversations with a mindset of collaboration rather than competition. Understanding the emotions behind someone's financial decisions allows you to work together toward mutually beneficial solutions.

4. Cultivate Resilience

Resilience is the ability to bounce back from setbacks, which is crucial for financial success. Everyone faces financial challenges at some point, whether it's a job loss, a failed investment, or unexpected expenses. Emotional resilience helps you recover from these setbacks with optimism and determination.

How to Cultivate Resilience:

- Reframe financial failures as learning opportunities. Instead of dwelling on what went wrong, focus on what you can learn and how to improve moving forward.
- Develop a positive self-talk habit. When facing financial challenges, remember that setbacks are temporary and you have the strength to overcome them. This will build emotional resilience and keep you moving toward your financial goals.

Aligning Emotions with Financial Goals

Aligning your emotions with your financial goals is about creating harmony between how you feel about money and what you want to achieve.

Your actions naturally follow suit when your emotions are aligned with abundance, confidence, and gratitude. You make smarter financial decisions, recognize more opportunities, and attract remarkable success.

Here's how to align your emotions with your financial goals:

1. Visualize Financial Success

Visualization is a powerful tool for aligning your emotions with your goals. Take time each day to visualize yourself achieving your financial goals. Picture the specific outcomes you want to create—whether it's paying off debt, buying a home, or building a successful business. As you visualize, focus on the emotions you will feel when you achieve these goals: joy, gratitude, security, and pride. These emotions reinforce your belief in financial abundance and help you stay motivated.

2. Practice Emotional Calibration

Emotional calibration involves checking in with your emotions regularly to ensure they are aligned with your financial goals. For example, if you want to build wealth, ask yourself throughout the day, "Do my current emotions align with abundance or scarcity?" If you notice fear or doubt creeping in, use the emotional regulation techniques discussed earlier to shift your emotional state.

3. Surround Yourself with Positive Emotional Influences

The people you surround yourself with significantly impact your emotional state. If you spend time with people who constantly worry about money or complain about financial problems, it's easy to absorb that negativity. Instead, seek out people with a positive, abundant mindset about money. Their confidence and optimism will rub off on you, helping you stay aligned with your financial goals.

Mastering Your Emotions for Financial Success

Emotional mastery is the foundation of financial success. When you learn to recognize, manage, and align your emotions with your financial goals, you can make empowered decisions that lead to greater wealth and abundance. Remember, emotions are not your enemy—they are powerful tools that, when harnessed correctly, can help you achieve your dreams. By practicing emotional regulation techniques, developing emotional intelligence, and aligning your feelings with abundance, you set yourself up for a prosperous financial future.

In the next chapter, we will explore how to apply the emotional mastery you've developed to specific financial strategies that accelerate wealth creation and help you stay on track for long-term success.

CHAPTER 9

Intuition and Money Tapping into Your Inner Wealth Guide

Many people focus solely on logic, analysis, and data when making financial decisions. While these are essential aspects of financial planning, intuition is another powerful tool often overlooked. Intuition is that inner voice, that gut feeling, guiding you to make decisions that align with your more profound understanding of what's right for you. Cultivating and trusting your intuition can complement logical financial planning, leading to more informed and empowered wealth-building choices.

This chapter will explore how intuition can be a valuable asset in your financial life. You'll learn how to cultivate and strengthen your intuitive abilities, balance intuition with logic, and use your inner wealth guide to decide about money, investments, and opportunities. By the end of this chapter, you will be equipped with practical exercises to help you tap into your financial intuition and create a more holistic approach to wealth creation.

The Power of Intuition in Financial Decision-Making

Intuition is often described as understanding something immediately without conscious reasoning. It's a feeling or a sense that arises from within, guiding you to the right decision, even if you can't logically explain why. While many people associate intuition with creativity or personal relationships, it also plays a crucial role in financial decision-making.

Intuition offers a different perspective in the financial world, where data, trends, and numbers dominate. It allows you to tap into your subconscious mind—where experiences, patterns, and past knowledge are stored—and make decisions that align with your deepest values and desires. Intuition is often shaped by a combination of past experiences, emotional intelligence, and understanding subtle cues that may not be immediately obvious through logic alone.

Why Intuition is Valuable in Money Matters

1. **Seeing Beyond Data**: While numbers and analysis are critical, they don't always tell the whole story. Intuition allows you to perceive opportunities or risks that data might overlook. It can alert you to potential problems before they become apparent or help you recognize a promising investment based on a gut feeling.

2. **Tapping into Emotional Wisdom**: Financial decisions are not always purely logical. They often involve emotions like fear, excitement, and hope. Intuition taps into emotional intelligence, helping you understand how a financial decision might align with your emotional state and long-term desires.

3. **Decision-Making in Uncertain Situations**: Not all financial decisions come with clear-cut data or perfect information. Intuition can guide you in uncertain or ambiguous situations when logic alone isn't enough. For example, when deciding whether to invest in a new business or buy a property, intuition might offer valuable insights that analysis alone can't provide.

Cultivating and Trusting Your Financial Intuition

While intuition is a natural ability, it can be strengthened and honed like any other skill. The key to developing financial intuition is learning to listen to that inner voice and trusting it when making decisions. Many people dismiss their intuition because it doesn't come with concrete evidence, but by cultivating it and using it alongside logic, you can create a more balanced approach to money.

1. Listen to Your Body's Signals

Intuition often manifests physically before it becomes a conscious thought. Your body can tell you whether a decision feels right or wrong. For example, when faced with a financial decision, you might feel a sense of ease or excitement if it aligns with your intuition. Conversely, you might feel tense, anxious, or unsettled if the decision goes against your intuitive guidance.

How to Tune into Your Body's Intuition:

- When making a financial decision, pause momentarily and notice how your body feels. Are you calm and relaxed, or do you feel tightness or discomfort? Pay attention to these subtle signals, often indicators of your intuition at work.
- If a financial opportunity excites you but also makes you feel uneasy, take a moment to explore why. Are you excited by the potential but nervous about the risk? Understanding the difference between excitement and anxiety can help you discern whether to move forward or pause.

2. Reflect on Past Intuitive Experiences

One way to build trust in your intuition is to reflect on past decisions where you followed (or ignored) your gut feeling. This reflection helps you recognize how your intuition has guided you in the past, reinforcing your confidence in it.

Exercise:

- Think of a time when you followed your intuition in a financial decision, whether it was making an investment, accepting a job offer, or saving money for a specific reason. How did the decision turn out? What signals or feelings led you to that decision?
- Now, think of a time when you ignored your intuition. How did that decision turn out? Were there subtle cues you missed or dismissed at the time? Reflecting on positive and negative outcomes will help you become more aware of your intuitive insights in future decisions.

3. Create Space for Intuition

In today's fast-paced world, getting caught up in distractions and external noise is easy, which can drown out your inner voice. To cultivate intuition, it's important to create moments of stillness where you can connect with your more profound wisdom.

How to Create Space for Intuition:

- Set aside time each day for quiet reflection or meditation. During this time, focus on a financial decision you're currently facing and allow your mind to process it without external inputs. Don't force a solution—sit with the decision and observe any thoughts, feelings, or ideas that arise.
- Engage in activities encouraging intuition, such as journaling, walking in nature, or practicing mindfulness. These activities help quiet the analytical mind and allow intuitive insights to emerge.

Balancing Intuition with Logical Financial Planning

While intuition is a powerful guide, it's most effective when used in tandem with logic and analysis. Combining intuition and data-driven planning creates a balanced approach that allows you to make informed financial decisions while trusting your inner guide.

1. Start with Research, Then Tune In

For any significant financial decision, start by gathering the necessary information. Whether researching an investment, evaluating a business opportunity, or reviewing your budget, use logic and analysis to understand the numbers. Once you have the facts, take a step back and check in with your intuition.

How to Combine Logic and Intuition:

- After researching, ask yourself: "What is my gut feeling about this?" If the data aligns with your intuition, that's a strong signal to move forward. If there's a disconnect between what the data suggests and what your intuition feels, take more time to reflect before deciding.
- Don't rush into decisions if your intuition is sending mixed signals. Sometimes, the data might look great, but something feels off. In these cases, further exploring the logical and intuitive aspects is worth exploring.

2. Trust the Timing of Intuition

One of the challenges of following intuition is that it doesn't always operate on a clear timeline. You might have a strong gut feeling about investing in something but don't have all the information yet. You might be ready to act logically, but your intuition tells you to wait, and you can trust that your intuition will guide you when the timing is right.

How to Trust Timing:

- Practice patience when making financial decisions. If you feel uncertain or if your intuition is nudging you to pause, give yourself time to process. Don't force decisions based solely on external pressures.
- If your intuition tells you to act quickly on an opportunity, listen to that impulse. Sometimes, intuition picks up on things your conscious mind hasn't fully recognized yet, such as a market shift or a window of opportunity closing.

Exercises to Strengthen Financial Intuition

Just as you would train a muscle, you can train your intuition regularly. The more you engage with your intuitive side, the more it develops and becomes a reliable guide in your financial life. Here are some exercises to help you strengthen your financial intuition:

Exercise 1: Daily Intuition Check-In

This simple exercise will help you build the habit of checking in with your intuition regularly.

1. Each morning, take five minutes to sit quietly and reflect on any financial decisions or opportunities on your mind.
2. Ask yourself: "What does my intuition say about this?" Pay attention to any feelings, images, or thoughts that arise. Don't judge them—observe.

3. Over time, you'll become more attuned to your intuition's subtle cues, making incorporating those insights into your financial planning easier.

Exercise 2: The "Yes" or "No" Game

This exercise helps you practice listening to your gut feelings when making quick decisions.

1. Think of a small financial decision you must make, such as purchasing something, investing a small amount, or saving money for a particular reason.
2. Close your eyes and ask yourself: "Is this a 'yes' or a 'no' for me right now?" Don't analyze—feel the answer in your body.
3. Practice this exercise with low-stakes decisions to build trust in your intuitive responses. Over time, you can apply it to more significant financial choices.

Exercise 3: Reflect on Your Dreams

Your subconscious mind often communicates through dreams, offering insights into your emotions, desires, and decisions. Keeping a dream journal can help you access your deeper intuition.

1. Daily, write down any dreams you remember, paying particular attention to symbols, feelings, or images related to money or success.
2. Reflect on how these dreams might connect to your financial situation. Dreams can offer valuable insights into your intuitive feelings about economic risks, opportunities, or concerns.

Final Thoughts: Integrating Intuition into Your Financial Journey

Cultivating and trusting your intuition is a powerful way to enhance financial decision-making. While logic and analysis provide essential data and structure, your intuition taps into a deeper wisdom that can guide you toward financial opportunities aligned with your personal goals and values. When you learn to balance both—combining careful planning with intuitive insights—you create a more holistic and confident approach to building wealth.

Remember, intuition is not about making impulsive decisions but listening to that inner voice that often knows more than your conscious mind can grasp. Practicing the exercises in this chapter will strengthen your connection to your inner wealth guide and help you learn to trust your instincts when making financial decisions.

As you continue your financial journey, integrate intuition into your process. Whether you're investing, planning for retirement, or making every day financial choices, trust that your intuition, when paired with logic, can lead to decisions that support your long-term success. Financial intuition can become one of your most valuable tools in creating a life of abundance and security.

In the next chapter, we will delve into how to take your newfound financial intuition and use it to develop proactive strategies for maximizing opportunities and navigating financial risks. With both logic and intuition working in harmony, you'll be well-equipped to face any financial challenge with confidence.

CHAPTER 10

The Awakened Mindset Living in Alignment with Abundance

As you've journeyed through this book, you've explored the deep connection between your mindset, emotions, and financial reality. You've learned to recognize the unconscious patterns that may have limited your financial success, and you've begun reprogramming your mind to embrace abundance. Now, in this final chapter, it's time to focus on how to make the awakened, empowered money mindset a natural part of your daily life. This is not just a temporary shift but a lasting transformation that leads to continuous growth and alignment with your highest financial potential.

This chapter will summarize the evolution from unconscious financial habits to an awakened mindset, guide how to maintain wealth consciousness and offer practical steps to ensure you live in alignment with abundance. Ultimately, this is your invitation to embrace an abundant mindset fully and to commit to a life of financial empowerment and freedom.

The Journey from Unconscious Financial Habits to an Awakened Money Mindset

The path to financial empowerment begins with awareness. Most people make economic decisions based on unconscious habits formed early in life. These habits are shaped by cultural conditioning, family beliefs, and personal experiences with money—often without any conscious choice. As a result, many people operate on autopilot, making financial choices driven by scarcity, fear, or old, limiting beliefs.

But awareness changes everything.

Throughout this journey, you've learned to:

- **Recognize Limiting Beliefs**: You've identified the beliefs that have held you back, such as "money is hard to come by" or "I'll never be wealthy." These beliefs were likely inherited or developed over time, but they no longer serve you.
- **Reprogram Your Subconscious Mind**: By using visualization, affirmations, and subconscious rewiring techniques, you've begun to replace old, scarcity-based beliefs with new, empowering ones. You now believe that wealth is possible, that abundance flows naturally into your life, and that you deserve financial success.
- **Align Your Emotions with Abundance**: You've learned how your emotions influence your financial decisions and developed the ability to regulate them. Now, emotions like gratitude, confidence, and joy guide your financial choices while fear, anxiety, and doubt have diminished.
- **Trust Your Intuition**: You've tapped into your inner wisdom to make intuitive financial decisions, complementing the logic and data that traditionally guide your financial life. This has allowed you to create a balanced, holistic approach to money.

The result of all this inner work is an **awakened money mindset**—a state of mind in which you are consciously aware of your financial habits and beliefs and actively shape your financial reality through positive thought patterns, emotions, and actions. You've gone from reacting unconsciously to money to actively creating your financial destiny.

Maintaining the Awakened Money Mindset on a Daily Basis

Achieving an awakened money mindset is a powerful accomplishment, but maintaining it is where the real transformation happens. The mind tends to revert to old habits, especially in times of stress or uncertainty, so developing daily practices that align your mindset with abundance is essential.

Here are key strategies to help you maintain your awakened mindset and wealth consciousness:

1. Daily Affirmations and Visualization

Consistency is key to maintaining a wealth mindset. Starting each day with a clear intention and focusing on abundance sets the tone for the rest of the day.

- **Affirmations**: Begin each morning with positive affirmations reinforcing your belief in abundance. For example, "I am a magnet for wealth and opportunities," or "Money flows to me easily and effortlessly." These affirmations shape your thoughts and train your subconscious mind to expect abundance.
- **Visualization**: Spend a few minutes each day visualizing your financial goals. See yourself achieving wealth, making smart investments, and living in economic freedom. The clearer your vision, the more your brain works to bring that vision into reality. Visualization activates the brain's neural pathways associated with goal achievement, making it easier for you to act in alignment with your desired outcomes.

2. Practice Gratitude

Gratitude is a powerful emotion that shifts one's focus from lack to abundance. When one focuses on what one already has, one sends a signal to the universe (and to one's subconscious mind) that one is ready to receive more.

- **Daily Gratitude Practice**: Write down three things you are grateful for each day, specifically money and abundance. This could include things like having a roof over your head, being able to pay your bills, or receiving an unexpected financial blessing. The more you focus on what's going well, the more you attract similar positive experiences.

Gratitude opens your mind to new opportunities and keeps you in a state of abundance, even when faced with challenges.

3. Be Mindful of Your Financial Decisions

Living with an awakened mindset means being intentional with your financial choices. Instead of making impulsive or fear-based decisions, pause and reflect on how your choices align with your long-term financial goals.

- **Mindful Spending**: Before making a purchase or financial decision, ask yourself: "Is this in alignment with my goals and values? Will this contribute to my financial growth, or is it a short-term indulgence?" This practice helps you make choices that reflect your abundance mindset rather than reacting from a place of scarcity.
- **Financial Planning**: Regularly review your financial goals and progress. Are you saving enough, investing wisely, and staying on track with your long-term plans? Taking a proactive approach to managing your money ensures you align with your financial vision.

4. Surround Yourself with Abundance-Minded People

The people you spend time with have a significant impact on your mindset. If you're surrounded by individuals who complain about money or live with a scarcity mentality, it's easy to absorb those negative beliefs. Instead, seek out people who share your abundance mindset—people who believe in growth, possibility, and financial freedom.

- **Find a Supportive Community**: Whether you join a mastermind group, attend seminars, or engage with mentors, surround yourself with people who inspire you to reach your financial potential. Conversations with like-minded individuals reinforce your commitment to abundance and help you focus on your goals.

5. Embrace Lifelong Learning

An awakened mindset is not a destination—it's an ongoing journey of growth and expansion. To maintain your abundance mindset, commit to continuous learning and personal development. The more you expand your knowledge about money, investments, and personal growth, the more empowered you'll feel.

- **Invest in Education**: Continue learning about wealth-building strategies, whether through books, courses, or mentorship. The more informed you are, the better equipped you'll be to make smart financial decisions.
- **Adapt and Evolve**: The financial world is constantly changing, and so should your approach to wealth. Stay open to new ideas, opportunities, and strategies. Flexibility is key to maintaining long-term financial success.

Living in Alignment with Your New Beliefs and Emotions

Living in alignment with your awakened mindset means that your thoughts, emotions, and actions are consistently aligned with abundance. You no longer operate from a place of fear, scarcity, or doubt—instead, you approach life with confidence, trust, and a deep belief in your ability to create wealth.

Aligning Thoughts with Abundance

Your thoughts shape your reality. By consistently thinking abundant thoughts, you align your mind with the energy of wealth. This doesn't mean ignoring financial challenges, but rather approaching them from a place of possibility rather than fear.

- **Catch Negative Thoughts**: When scarcity-based thoughts arise, such as "I can't afford this" or "There's never enough," pause and reframe them. Replace them with affirmations like "I can find a way to afford this" or "Opportunities for wealth are everywhere."

Aligning Emotions with Wealth

Your emotional state is a powerful magnet for attracting or repelling wealth. When you feel confident, joyful, and grateful, you raise your vibrational frequency to align with abundance. Conversely, emotions like fear, anxiety, or frustration lower your vibration and can block financial opportunities.

- **Emotional Regulation**: Use emotional mastery techniques to stay aligned with positive emotions. When negative emotions arise, such as fear about money, practice deep breathing, mindfulness, or emotional reframing to shift your emotional state back to abundance.

Aligning Actions with Your Financial Goals

Finally, your actions must align with your financial vision. Every decision you make, whether it's how you spend your money or how you invest your time, should move you closer to your goals.

- **Take Consistent Action**: Wealth-building is not a one-time event—it's the result of consistent, daily actions. Whether it's saving, investing, or learning a new skill, every action you take should reflect your commitment to financial abundance.

Final Call to Action: Embrace the Mindset of Abundance

As you end this journey, you've equipped yourself with the tools, strategies, and mindset needed to create financial success. But the journey doesn't end here—this is just the beginning. The true power of the awakened mindset comes when you fully commit to living in alignment with abundance, not just for a day, a week, or a month, but for the rest of your life.

- **Embrace Growth**: Continue expanding your wealth consciousness by applying what you've learned and remaining open to new opportunities for growth. Wealth is not static; it evolves as you evolve.
- **Trust Your Power**: You can create your financial reality. Trust in your ability to make decisions that lead to wealth and believe in your potential to achieve financial freedom.
- **Stay Aligned**: Align your thoughts, emotions, and actions with your desired wealth. When challenges arise, remember that your mindset is the key to overcoming them. Trust in your journey, stay committed to your financial vision, and consistently align with your goals.

This awakened mindset of abundance will transform your relationship with money and ripple into every area of your life. You'll experience more opportunities, deeper fulfillment, and greater confidence in navigating the financial world.

Conclusion: The Path Forward

You've learned to break free from limiting beliefs, align your emotions with abundance, reprogram your subconscious mind for wealth, and trust your intuition. As you move forward, remember that financial success is a continuous journey of growth, learning, and evolution.

Your mindset is your most valuable asset—nurture, protect, and allow it to guide you to the financial freedom you deserve. Embrace abundance in all areas of your life, and let your awakened mindset lead you to new levels of success, fulfillment, and prosperity.

The world is full of wealth and opportunity, and it's yours for the taking.

BONUS CHAPTER

BITCOIN The Digital Revolution of Money and Wealth Creation

Bitcoin has transformed the financial landscape, becoming one of the most significant innovations in the modern economic world. While it began as a fringe technology primarily used by tech enthusiasts, it has now evolved into a mainstream asset class and a key component of conversations around money, decentralization, and financial independence.

In this chapter, we'll explore Bitcoin's origins, how it works, and why it's become such a powerful tool for wealth creation. We'll also discuss how to invest in Bitcoin and use it to hedge against financial loss while considering the risks and volatility associated with this digital currency.

The Origins and Power of Bitcoin

Bitcoin was introduced in 2009 by an anonymous entity known as Satoshi Nakamoto. It was developed as a peer-to-peer electronic cash system without any centralized authority, such as banks or governments. Instead, Bitcoin operates on a decentralized ledger technology called blockchain, which records every transaction across a network of computers.

Bitcoin is revolutionary because it is finite; only 21 million Bitcoins will ever be created. This scarcity is part of what makes it so valuable, and it offers a decentralized alternative to traditional fiat currencies.

Bitcoin's unique features, such as its resistance to censorship and inflation, have made it an appealing option for those looking to escape the traditional financial system's limitations. Over the years, it has evolved from a niche digital currency to a widely accepted store of value—often referred to as "digital gold."

Using Bitcoin as a Hedge Against Losses

One of Bitcoin's most attractive features for investors is its potential to hedge against traditional market risks. While conventional assets like stocks and bonds are influenced by inflation, political instability, and financial crises, Bitcoin's decentralized nature makes it less susceptible to these risks.

Investors often see Bitcoin as a hedge against inflation and currency devaluation. In countries where the national currency has lost value due to hyperinflation, Bitcoin has become a preferred method of preserving wealth. This is because, unlike fiat currency, Bitcoin cannot be printed endlessly, thus maintaining its scarcity and value over time.

Furthermore, Bitcoin's independence from traditional financial systems allows it to thrive even during economic downturns. In fact, some investors buy Bitcoin specifically during times of crisis to protect their portfolios from larger market drops.

How to Invest in Bitcoin

Investing in Bitcoin has become increasingly accessible in recent years, and you can incorporate it into your wealth-building strategy in several ways.

1. **Direct Purchase**: The most straightforward way to invest in Bitcoin is to buy it directly through a cryptocurrency exchange like Coinbase, Binance, or Kraken. After purchase, you can store your Bitcoin in a digital wallet, online or offline, for increased security.
2. **Bitcoin ETFs and Funds**: For those looking to invest in Bitcoin without directly holding it, Bitcoin exchange-traded funds (ETFs) and investment funds provide a less technical entry point. These funds allow you to invest in Bitcoin without worrying about wallets, private keys, or other cryptocurrency management aspects.
3. **Dollar-Cost Averaging (DCA)**: If you're concerned about Bitcoin's volatility, dollar-cost averaging is a smart strategy. This involves investing a fixed amount of money in Bitcoin at regular intervals, which helps reduce the impact of market fluctuations and averages out the price over time.
4. **Bitcoin Mining**: Though it requires significant computational power and energy, mining Bitcoin is another way to gain exposure. However, this method is more suited for tech-savvy individuals or those with access to low-cost energy solutions.

Making Money with Bitcoin

Bitcoin's meteoric rise in value over the past decade has made it one of the most profitable investments for early adopters. However, there are several ways you can leverage Bitcoin to grow your wealth today:

1. **Long-Term Holding (HODLing)**: Many Bitcoin investors buy and hold their Bitcoin, trusting in its long-term appreciation. Despite its short-term volatility, Bitcoin has historically trended upward, making HODLing a popular strategy.

2. **Trading**: For more experienced investors, actively trading Bitcoin can be highly profitable. Bitcoin's volatility allows traders to profit from price fluctuations, though it requires a deep understanding of technical analysis and market trends.

3. **Earning Interest on Bitcoin**: Several platforms allow you to lend out your Bitcoin and earn interest. This way, rather than just holding Bitcoin, you can generate passive income on your investment.

4. **Participating in Bitcoin Forks and Airdrops**: Occasionally, Bitcoin undergoes forks or network upgrades that create new cryptocurrencies. Holders of Bitcoin may receive free coins (airdrops) from these events, which can be sold or held as additional investments.

The Risks of Bitcoin

Despite its potential for wealth creation, Bitcoin is not without risks. Its volatility is legendary—prices can swing by double digits in a single day, making it a high-risk, high-reward investment.

Additionally, while Bitcoin is becoming more widely accepted, it still faces regulatory uncertainty. Governments worldwide are still determining how to regulate Bitcoin and other cryptocurrencies, which could impact their value and legality.

Lastly, as with any digital asset, there's a risk of cyberattacks. It's crucial to store Bitcoin securely, whether in a hardware or highly secure digital wallet.

Final Thoughts: Bitcoin's Role in Your Financial Future

Bitcoin offers incredible potential as both a hedge against traditional financial risks and a tool for wealth creation. While it requires careful consideration and management, it can be a valuable addition to your portfolio, particularly if you're looking for ways to diversify and protect your wealth from economic uncertainty.

As with any investment, it's essential to thoroughly research, understand the risks, and invest only what you can afford to lose. Bitcoin represents a digital revolution in money, and as the world continues to move toward decentralization and digital assets, its role in wealth-building will only grow stronger.

Bonus 2: 7-Day Mindset Awakening Action Plan

This 7-Day Mindset Awakening Action Plan is designed to help you solidify and integrate everything you've learned throughout this book. Over the next week, you'll focus on daily actions that will awaken your money mindset and align your thoughts, emotions, and behaviors with abundance. Each day's action builds upon the previous one, creating a foundation for lasting financial transformation.

Day 1: Clarify Your Financial Vision

Objective: Set a powerful financial vision to guide your decisions and actions.

- **Action**: Take 20-30 minutes to sit quietly and visualize your ideal financial future. Where are you in five or ten years? What does financial freedom look like for you? Be as specific as possible—consider your income, lifestyle, investments, and feelings about money.

Write this vision in detail, including the emotions you associate with achieving it.
- **Bonus Tip**: Create a vision board or digital collage representing your financial goals. Place it somewhere you can see every day to reinforce your vision.

Day 2: Identify and Release Limiting Beliefs

Objective: Break free from old, scarcity-driven beliefs about money.

- **Action**: Write down any limiting beliefs you still hold about money, such as "I'll never have enough," "Money is hard to come by," or "I'm not good with finances." Once identified, challenge these beliefs by reframing them into empowering, abundance-focused statements. For example, replace "I'll never have enough" with "There is always more than enough for me."
- **Bonus Tip**: Use affirmations to reinforce your new beliefs throughout the day. Say them out loud or write them down when you feel negative thoughts creeping in.

Day 3: Practice Gratitude for Abundance

Objective: Shift your focus from lack to abundance by recognizing the wealth already present in your life.

- **Action**: Begin a daily gratitude practice focused on money. Write down at least three things you are grateful for regarding your finances, no matter how small. This could be paying a bill, receiving a paycheck, or accessing financial resources like books or mentors.
- **Bonus Tip**: As you go through your day, pause and mentally express gratitude whenever you spend or

receive money. This keeps you aligned with abundance even in daily transactions.

Day 4: Cultivate Financial Intuition

Objective: Strengthen your financial intuition and trust in your inner wealth guide.

- **Action**: Spend 10 minutes meditating on a financial decision or opportunity you currently face. Quiet your mind, focus on your breath, and ask your intuition for guidance. Pay attention to any feelings, thoughts, or insights that arise, even if they initially don't seem logical.
- **Bonus Tip**: Start a financial intuition journal where you record intuitive insights you receive during the day. This helps you track how your intuition guides you over time.

Day 5: Take Inspired Financial Action

Objective: Align your actions with your awakened mindset by moving toward your financial goals.

- **Action**: Take one inspired financial action today that brings you closer to your vision of abundance. This could be anything from investing in opening a savings account to researching wealth-building strategies to asking for a raise. Ensure this action aligns with your financial vision and is not fear driven.
- **Bonus Tip**: Visualize yourself succeeding and feeling confident about your steps before acting.

Day 6: Create Your Abundance Environment

Objective: Surround yourself with positive influences that reinforce your abundance mindset.

- **Action**: Declutter anything that symbolizes lack or negativity in your physical and digital spaces. This could include old financial documents that remind you of debt or anything that doesn't support your wealth goals. Replace these with symbols of abundance, such as books on wealth, uplifting financial mentors, or affirmations.
- **Bonus Tip**: Curate your social media feeds to focus on wealth-building content. Follow people who inspire you and remove accounts that make you feel limited or stressed about money.

Day 7: Reflect and Celebrate Your Growth

Objective: Reflect on your progress and celebrate your shifts toward an abundance mindset.

- **Action**: Take time to reflect on the week's exercises. Write down the most significant insights or breakthroughs you've experienced and how your mindset has shifted. Celebrate the progress you've made, even if it feels small. Acknowledge yourself for taking steps toward a wealthier, more empowered future.
- **Bonus Tip**: Based on your awakened mindset, set new financial goals. These goals should be bigger and more ambitious, reflecting your newfound confidence and alignment with abundance.

Conclusion: Your Path Forward

This 7-Day Mindset Awakening Action Plan is just the beginning. As you continue to implement these daily actions, your financial mindset will become more natural and aligned with abundance. The key is consistency—repeating these practices reinforces the beliefs, emotions, and actions that lead to long-term financial success.

The journey to wealth begins in the mind. Stay committed to your growth, trust in your ability to create financial freedom, and continue building an abundant future.

A Personal Note from Choyo Gomex

As you reach the final pages of this journey, I want to take a moment to thank you sincerely. Together, we explored powerful ideas, challenged limiting beliefs, and embraced new ways of thinking about wealth and abundance. This book is a labor of love, written to help you unlock the potential that's always been within you.

If the lessons in these pages have resonated with you, sparked an "aha!" moment, or inspired real changes in your life, I would be eternally grateful if you shared your thoughts in a review on Amazon. Your review isn't just feedback—it's a way for others who may be searching for the same answers you once were to discover this work. Your voice matters, and I would love for others to hear it, too. Whether it's your favorite chapter, a breakthrough moment, or how this book has shifted your mindset, your insights can help others find their own path to abundance.

Thank you for reading, growing, and participating in this journey. The world of financial freedom is vast and full of possibilities—here's to your continued success and the exciting road ahead.

With deep gratitude,

Choyo Gomex

A Heartfelt Farewell to the Triad Series

As we reach the final pages of this book—and indeed, the last installment in the *Money Triad Series*—I want to take a moment to express my deep gratitude to you, the reader. You've embarked on a transformative journey, and I'm honored that you've allowed these books to guide you through this powerful process of awakening your mindset and embracing financial freedom.

This journey, from unconscious habits to mastery over your financial destiny, has not been a short one. You've explored the universal principles of wealth, learned to reprogram your financial beliefs, and now stand empowered, aligned with an abundant mindset. But this is not the end—it is, in fact, the beginning of a lifelong relationship with wealth, abundance, and freedom.

A Reflection on the Journey: The Money Triad Series

This final book, *Money Mindset Awakened: Your Guide to Achieve Next-Level Financial Freedom*, was written as the culmination of everything we've explored together. The *Money Triad Series* has been a step-by-step blueprint to unlock your financial potential, each book representing a different growth phase. Let's take a moment to reflect on the entire series and what each part of this journey represents.

Book One: *Money: The Universal Language of Wealth*

In *Money: The Universal Language of Wealth*, we explored the fundamental principles of money itself. This book was your introduction to understanding how wealth operates as a language spoken universally, regardless of background or circumstances. The goal was to demystify money and remove any fear or confusion. We delved into the mechanics of wealth and how to leverage it to create the financial future you deserve.

This book was about laying a foundation—a solid understanding of how wealth flows and how you can tap into that flow. It aimed to make money less intimidating and more accessible, showing you that the language of wealth is not reserved for the elite, but for anyone willing to learn and apply it.

Book Two: *The Money Blueprint: Your Guide to Master Wealth and Prosperity*

The Money Blueprint: Your Guide to Master Wealth and Prosperity took things a step further. Here, we explored the mental and emotional frameworks that shape your financial reality. We examined the subconscious beliefs, behaviors, and patterns influencing your financial decisions. Through practical exercises, affirmations, and step-by-step guidance, this book helped you design and implement a personalized financial blueprint that aligned with your goals for prosperity.

In this phase of your journey, you learned to recognize the internal roadblocks to wealth and to reprogram them with powerful, prosperity-focused beliefs. This book showed you that wealth isn't just something you work for—it's something you can program into your life. It's about building the foundation of wealth from the inside out.

Book Three: *Money Mindset Awakened: Your Guide to Achieve Next-Level Financial Freedom*

Finally, in *Money Mindset Awakened*, we've moved beyond the basics and entered the realm of mastery. This book has been about aligning your thoughts, emotions, and actions with the energy of abundance on a daily basis. You've learned to create wealth and live in harmony with it here. You've discovered how to use tools like emotional intelligence, visualization, and intuition to become fully empowered in your financial life.

This final chapter of the *Money Triad Series* brings everything full circle. It's not just about understanding money or creating wealth—it's about maintaining a state of financial empowerment for the rest of your life. You no longer chase money by cultivating these habits, mindset shifts, and emotional tools. Instead, you've become a magnet for wealth, drawing it toward you effortlessly.

Moving Forward: Your Journey Continues

As we close this chapter, it's essential to recognize that while this may be the end of the *Money Triad Series*, your journey toward financial mastery is far from over. Wealth and abundance are not destinations—they are ongoing experiences. The principles you've learned through this series will continue to grow, evolve, and manifest in new ways as you apply them to your daily life.

I encourage you to return to these books often. The knowledge and insights within are timeless; as your life changes, you'll find new lessons and deeper meanings in the words. Whether you revisit a specific chapter that resonated with you or use one of the exercises to get back on track, these tools are here for you as long as you need them.

But remember, you are already empowered. You've already laid the groundwork; now, it's about maintaining your alignment with abundance. Keep your wealth mindset strong by practicing daily habits reinforcing your goals, surround yourself with people who uplift and inspire you, and always stay open to growth.

A Call to Embrace Abundance

So, here is my final call to action: embrace abundance in every area of your life. It's not just about financial wealth; it's about living with an open heart, a curious mind, and a willingness to receive all the good life offers. Embrace growth. Embrace challenges as opportunities for expansion. Embrace the limitless potential within you to create the life you dream of.

As you move forward, remember that your financial journey is deeply personal. There is no one-size-fits-all formula for wealth, but you now have the tools, mindset, and strategies to create your own path. Trust yourself. Trust the knowledge you've gained and trust the power of your mind to shape your financial reality.

Closing the Chapter on the Money Series

Writing the *Money Triad Series* has also been an amazing journey for me. Each book has been crafted to empower you, the reader, to realize that financial freedom is not just possible—it's inevitable when you align your mindset and actions with abundance.

I want to thank you personally for allowing me to be part of your journey. Whether this is the first book you've read or you've been with me since the beginning, know that your success and growth have always been my driving force. You can achieve extraordinary things, and I can't wait to see the abundance you'll create in your life.

In closing, I leave you with this: wealth is your birthright. You are worthy of every dream, opportunity, and form of success that comes your way. Continue to grow, expand, and live in alignment with the limitless abundance that surrounds you.

Thank you again for being part of this journey.

To your continued success, abundance, and freedom.

Regards,
Choyo Gomex

Hello Empowered Reader

Congratulations on completing *Money Mindset Awakened: The Key to Achieving Next-Level Wealth*! You've embarked on a transformative journey to reshape your financial mindset and unlock your full potential for wealth and abundance. Your dedication to mastering the mental aspects of financial success is truly inspiring.

As a token of appreciation for your commitment to financial growth, I'm excited to offer you an exclusive **45-minute one-on-one personalized coaching session via Zoom at no cost**. This session will provide you with tailored guidance to deepen your understanding of money mindset principles or address any specific questions related to your financial journey.

To claim your session, simply email me at **choyo@gomex.com** with the subject line "**Next Level Coaching**," and we'll schedule a time that works best for you.

Thank you for taking this significant step toward achieving lasting prosperity. I look forward to helping you further enhance your financial mindset and achieve your goals.

Wishing you continued success and abundance,

Choyo Gomex

REFERENCES

Books on Wealth Mindset and Financial Freedom

1) "Think and Grow Rich"

by Napoleon Hill

A classic text on the power of mindset and its role in achieving financial success. Hill's book remains a go-to guide for those wanting to understand the psychological principles behind wealth-building.

2) "The Millionaire Mind"

by Thomas J. Stanley

This book explores the habits and mindsets of millionaires, providing valuable insights into how financial success is achieved.

3) "You Are a Badass at Making Money"

by Jen Sincero

Sincero's book blends practical advice with personal empowerment, helping readers break through their financial blocks.

4) "Secrets of the Millionaire Mind"

by T. Harv Eker

Eker breaks down the mental patterns that separate the wealthy from those who struggle financially. His insights on wealth conditioning are particularly valuable for readers looking to rewire their subconscious beliefs.

5) "The Richest Man in Babylon"

by George S. Clason

A timeless classic that provides financial wisdom through parables set in ancient Babylon, offering simple yet profound lessons on saving, investing, and wealth-building.

Books on Neuroscience and Emotional Intelligence

1) "The Power of Habit"

by Charles Duhigg
This book explores the science of habit formation and how changing habits can lead to success in all areas of life, including finances.

2) "Emotional Intelligence"

by Daniel Goleman
Goleman's seminal work on emotional intelligence offers insights into how emotions shape our decision-making, including financial choices.

3) "Mindset: The New Psychology of Success"

by Carol S. Dweck
Dweck's groundbreaking research on fixed and growth mindsets helps explain how our beliefs about our abilities influence our success in all areas, including wealth creation.

4) "The Biology of Belief"

by Bruce H. Lipton
This book delves into how our beliefs, often subconscious, shape our lives on a cellular level and how we can reprogram them for success.

Books and Resources on Personal Growth and Visualization

1) "The Magic of Thinking Big"

by David J. Schwartz
This book emphasizes the importance of big thinking to achieve extraordinary success and how visualization can help unlock personal and financial growth.

2) **"Breaking the Habit of Being Yourself"**

by Dr. Joe Dispenza
Dispenza offers scientific explanations of how to break free from limiting beliefs through visualization, meditation, and other practical exercises.

3) **"The Dynamic Laws of Prosperity"**

by Catherine Ponder
A spiritual take on how prosperity and abundance are tied to mindset and belief systems, full of affirmations and techniques for cultivating wealth consciousness.

Articles and Studies

1) **"How Gratitude Changes You and Your Brain"**

by Joshua Brown and Joel Wong, *Greater Good Magazine*
This article explores the neuroscience behind gratitude and how it can rewire the brain to support more positive emotions and experiences, including wealth.

2) **"The Neuroscience of Financial Decision-Making"**

Harvard Business Review
This article provides insights into how the brain processes risk, reward, and decision-making in financial contexts.

3) **"The Science Behind Visualization: How It Can Help Achieve Your Goals"**

Psychology Today
A breakdown of the research supporting visualization practices and how they can enhance success across various aspects of life, including finances.

www.ingramcontent.com/pod-product-compliance
Lightning Source LLC
Chambersburg PA
CBHW050259230526
45471CB00005B/1957